THE
BUSINESS SIDE
OF A
SPIRITUAL
PRACTICE

A Marketing & Public Relations Guide
for the Spiritual Business

LINN RANDOM

BALBOA.PRESS
A DIVISION OF HAY HOUSE

Balboa Press books may be ordered through booksellers or by contacting:

Balboa Press
A Division of Hay House
1663 Liberty Drive
Bloomington, IN 47403
www.balboapress.com
1 (877) 407-4847

Because of the dynamic nature of the Internet, any web addresses or links contained in this book may have changed since publication and may no longer be valid. The views expressed in this work are solely those of the author and do not necessarily reflect the views of the publisher, and the publisher hereby disclaims any responsibility for them.

The author of this book does not dispense medical advice or prescribe the use of any technique as a form of treatment for physical, emotional, or medical problems without the advice of a physician, either directly or indirectly. The intent of the author is only to offer information of a general nature to help you in your quest for emotional and spiritual well-being. In the event you use any of the information in this book for yourself, which is your constitutional right, the author and the publisher assume no responsibility for your actions.

Any people depicted in stock imagery provided by Getty Images are models, and such images are being used for illustrative purposes only.
Certain stock imagery © Getty Images.

Scripture quotations marked KJV are from the Holy Bible, King James Version (Authorized Version). First published in 1611. Quoted from the KJV Classic Reference Bible, Copyright © 1983 by The Zondervan Corporation.

Print information available on the last page.

ISBN: 978-1-9822-4790-4 (sc)
ISBN: 978-1-9822-4791-1 (e)

Balboa Press rev. date: 05/13/2020

This book is dedicated to my teachers who inspired me James Van Praagh, Louise Hay, Dr. Roy Graves, Sal Jade and Dr. Richard Green.

To my son, Michael Vaught; my daughter-in-law, Elisabeth Walters; my sister, Sandra Napier; and my husband, Chris.

I also want to acknowledge the Archangels who work with me daily: Archangels Michael, Raphael, Metatron, Azrael, Ariel, and to all the Fairies and Guides who all have inspired me in life and along the way as I worked on this book.

This book is also dedicated to you, the reader, and your success.

CONTENTS

Part III: Marketing on the World Wide Web

Part IV: The Business Plan and Promotional Calendar

INTRODUCTION

A little over a year ago, I met with a group of psychics who had just finished their psychic development course.

It was graduation day for the group. They were gifted, trained, and all proudly held their certificates close to their hearts. They were bright-eyed and eager to start their respective spiritual practices.

I was delighted to speak to them. What a privilege! My presentation was "How to Market and Promote the Spiritual Practice." I anticipated my subject would be received with joy and gratitude. Instead, as I spoke, the glitter in their eyes gave way to sheer panic and anxiety. It was abundantly clear to me not one of the graduating students had considered the practical aspects of starting and marketing their new businesses, nor did they even know where to begin.

With a background in international marketing, I felt pressed by my Angels and Guides to write this book for those students and for you. This book will tell you how to make your business a success.

You have been directed by the Universe to use your gifts and talents in an ancient healing practice. Your mission is a mandate from the Divine to heal, empower, and change the planet for good.

This book is a primer on how and where to market your spiritual practice online and in the real world. It is a comprehensive guide that contains sound strategies on public relations, advertising, and promotions that will help you make your calling a spiritual and a financial success.

I will be providing you a lot of information in this book. Don't be overwhelmed. As you review opportunities, keep in mind, you can decide what aspects of marketing will best serve you, fit in your budget, and allows your company to grow and prosper.

For example, if you feel you have an aptitude for public speaking, you will find a chapter on how to take advantage of speaking opportunities. If public speaking is not your cup of tea, then choose another marketing or public-relations strategy that does appeal to you.

Remember Heaven is cheering you on! You came into this world to make a difference. Success is your birthright. You have been called to help others. You are immensely talented and possess a loving giving heart and beautiful spirit. You were meant to be in this business.

The Universe believes in you. I believe in you. I totally support your every dream.

PART 1

THE SPIRITUAL FOUNDATION

CHAPTER 1

BUILDING A SPIRITUAL FOUNDATION

Chinese philosopher Lao-tzu said a journey of a thousand miles begins with a single step. Welcome. You have taken that first step toward starting your own successful spiritual practice.

In this first section, let's talk about your readiness to start your own business by building a strong foundation for success. If your practice is already established but you feel there is something holding you back from experiencing greater success, we'll root out any fears, negative thoughts, beliefs, or anything else that could keep you from reaching that finish line, a successful spiritual practice.

If you feel you don't need a self-inventory, it's okay to move on to the next section. However, if you want to explore any personal demons hiding in the dark recesses of your heart, we're going to help you uncover anything standing between you and your success.

Businesses fail every day. That's not going to be you. God has a plan for you, and the Universe endowed you with gifts and abilities to help others. You are destined to change the world.

Let's begin this adventure by understanding what a successful business looks like for you. In order to achieve success, you need to have an idea of what success looks like and feels like to you. Now is the time to dream big.

You were drawn to start your own spiritual practice because there is a deep, innate need in you to help others. You are intuitive, talented, gifted, and knowledgeable in the New Age arts and ancient practices. You are now ready to turn your talents into a business. While you will receive great satisfaction from helping others, to be in business and stay in business, the landlord wants his due.

Teachers go into education because they have a passion to teach children. While this is certainly a rewarding and an altruistic career, the light bill still needs to be paid.

When I first began to write, I wanted to be a juvenile mystery author. I had a singular vision of one day finding my book in the library with a child having scribbled on the inside cover, "Read this! Good book!" As I grew, my genre changed, and so did my definition of personal success.

Today, my financial dream is to live debt-free in a home that is paid for. By the way, if I haven't thanked you for helping me achieve this dream by buying this book, I humbly thank you now!

Today, my passion is to make you a success. I want you to contemplate your image of success in full and complete detail.

Defining Your Success

As you contemplate your own practice, an important first step is to understand what success will look like to you. What does success feel like to you? Your emotions and your feelings must be in tune with your image of success.

Do you define success as a six-figure salary, a luxurious home with a pool, and frequent European vacations? Or does your definition of success mean living debt-free? How much money would you have in your bank account? What kind of car would you drive? Where would you live? You can have whatever you desire if your vision is clear and resonates within you.

Close your eyes, and visualize how you or your family will enjoy your success. Put as much thought and energic feeling into your desired outcome. Together, we are going to create a new language of success by capturing and internalizing your personal and financial goals.

This will mean you will stop listening to voices of teachers, parents, friends, and literally anyone who ever told you that you would not be successful or made you feel less than who you really are. Shut out the nonsensical self-talk that says you are too old, too young, too poor, or too unworthy to make your dream a reality. Let's make you the star of your own life. If no one has told you before, I will do so now. Success is and has always been your birthright.

Take a moment to write out your vision of success. Fill in every detail as you define your ideal of success. Have a clear vision of what kind of car you will drive and how it will feel driving that car. How much money will be in your checking and savings accounts? What does your neighborhood look like? From your mailbox, what does your home look like? Use the key in your hand and go to your front door. Open it, and walk through your home as you admire your furniture, your kitchen, your beautiful bathroom, and your bedrooms. Fill each room with photos, personal mementos, and your bookcases with books that inspire you and novels you enjoy. What does your home feel like? Embrace the warmth and welcoming feel to it.

Now turn to your spiritual practice. Do you have a home office or a retail location? Imagine what your practice area looks like. Do you fill your appointment book with page after page of appointments? How do your clients feel after a session with you? How do you feel at the end of a busy day?

Write down each thought, dream, and hope; this is your desired outcome, and you will breathe life into your vision.

Go back to this place daily, and know that I affirm your vision of success. This or something more manifests in your life. And so it is!

The next several chapters are written to explore anything that may hold you back from experiencing your success. Let's uncover any thought or any secret thing that could keep you from achieving this success. We are first going to look at the Ego.

CHAPTER 2

THE EGO

The word *Ego* comes from the Latin pronoun I. The Ego is the image we hold of ourselves. It's the sum total of who we think we are and sometimes gets blended with the perception of what others think of us.

When we use the words ego or egotistical, we generally think of them in unflattering terms used to describe someone who is vain, boastful, self-absorbed, and opinionated. We believe being called egotistical is unflattering in other people and certainly in ourselves.

There is another side to ego, for having little or no ego can be just as damaging and debilitating. This aspect of the ego says to the self, "I am unworthy. I do not deserve good, love, or success." This wearying sense of self says, "Why bother starting a business? I will never be successful at it anyway."

Words only hurt you if you believe they are true.

Everyone should have a healthy opinion of the self that is balanced, independent, and free from the opinions of others.

For many of us, low opinions of ourselves began in childhood when critical words were spoken to us by parents, teachers, or schoolyard bullies or perhaps simply materialized in the dark shadows of our own self-talk.

Feelings of unworthiness are as familiar to us as the lyrics of an old song that continuously plays in the background of our minds. Left unchecked, these longstanding melodies permeate every aspect of our lives. Feeling we're unworthy will keep us from our success. It will keep us from experiencing unlimited abundance, joy, and even love.

Feeling everyone is worthy of success but you will keep you trapped in a chasm of darkness. Believing success is an attainable goal for others but not yourself is a lie. Your choice is to remain in this dark pit of lies you have accepted for yourself or rise from distorted view of reality into the beautiful truth of who you truly are.

You are special, perfect, whole, and complete. These are not words to skim over as you read. Pause and dwell on them until you internalize them and feel them in every cell of your body, for they are who you really are.

Now would be a good time to write down your thoughts and feelings about success, truly knowing in your core that what men or women can conceive, they can achieve.

In sales and in life is an adage that says there are two reasons for doing anything: the real reason and the one that sounds good.

Your fear-born, false ego may be telling you that you will never be able to leave your dead-end job, as it is keeping a roof over your head. If you go deeper, you may discover the real reason for staying in that job is because your ego is saying you are not worthy of success. Once you acknowledge and understand the real reason you are not starting your practice, you will be able to adjust your course. Get to the real reason, and uncover what is holding you back.

There may be strong reasons for staying in that dead-end job temporarily, but you don't have to stay there forever. With planning, you can transition into your own successful spiritual practice. It's perfectly okay to begin your practice in baby steps before you take off running to a brighter future doing something you love and desire. Just be sure you are not being held back by the belief you must stay in your current situation forever, if there is something you would rather do.

The belief that you're not worthy is a lie. To rise above feelings of unworthiness, you must raise your self-esteem. Affirmations are wonderful, but you must believe those affirmations are true. To change your opinion of yourself, begin by writing down a list of attributes you like about yourself. This is your starting place.

Write down and appreciate the good, strong, kind qualities you possess. When I began this exercise for myself, I could only conceive of one good thing about myself. It took days and weeks before I could add to my list, but as I did, I saw the good qualities within me. I wasn't an ugly, victimized duckling after all. I found the beautiful swan within me and came to honor the girl I saw in the mirror. The good qualities were always there; I had such a low opinion of myself, it took me a while to find them.

Keep working on your list; fill up page after page as you acknowledge and understand who you truly are. Review your list and add to it every day. This is your mission to uncover who you really are, and as your list grows longer, so will your self-esteem and how you view yourself.

Love and appreciate yourself every day; make it your mission to do at least one nice thing for yourself every day. Make you the star of your own life!

Make a date with yourself to enjoy a walk, read a book that uplifts you, or take a long bath. Do whatever do need to do to make yourself feel special, because you are special. You deserve to know you are special and show it to yourself. Say *I am worthy* every minute of every day until you know it's true. I can absolutely assure you will uncover a higher version of yourself, one who deserves every aspect of success.

Live in a no-judgment zone. Stop judging others and yourself; this most certainly includes your past and your mistakes. Stop all negative talk. As you live in this no-judgment zone, the shackles of judging yourself and others will fall by the wayside, and you will feel lighter and freer.

Focus instead on wholly what makes you feel good and what enhances your life. You will only experience financial abundance when you internalize it and accept it for yourself.

As you uplift your sense of self, you will experience positive change in your world. Raise your thoughts, emotions, and vibrations; you will create a new life for yourself with a healthy, balanced ego.

Write down your accomplishments, affirmations, and your dreams. You will see what I see now—someone who deserves success. You were born into spiritual royalty with a manifest destiny to help and heal the world.

In your meditation and visualization work, see yourself as a confident, savvy businessman or -woman. See and feel your success, and watch as every dream come true. Your magical once upon a time is here now.

God will never give you a dream without fulfillment. Heaven wants you to succeed. Your first step is believing in you. I want you to know, I do.

CHAPTER 3

BELIEFS ABOUT MONEY

To understand your beliefs about money, I feel it is first important to understand how the laws of the Universe work within and around us. We live in a world governed by invisible laws. These invisible laws govern our planet.

For example, we cannot see or physically feel the Law of Gravity, and yet it is there and works the same for everyone. If you and I both drop a book, I promise you, both books will fall to the floor. It's the law.

We are reminded of the Law of Centrifugal force every time we drive our vehicles around a curve. If we do not adjust our automobiles to the speed and bend of the road, our vehicles will likely end up in a ditch.

The Law of Attraction is forever in play in our lives. Whatever we focus on, we bring into our experience. If you want good, love, and abundance, then fully focus on those ideals. The Universe will respond in accordance to your thoughts and feelings. If you focus on fear, lack, and the negative, the Universe will not only respond in kind, sometimes tenfold as whatever you send out comes back multiplied. The Universe is impartial and will respond to whatever we give our attention to.

There is an old song about how the rich get rich and the poor get children. The rich get rich because they focus on wealth and enjoying the pleasures money can buy. The poor who are focused on lack will reap the corresponding experiences. It's the law.

The Universe will give you exactly what you focus on, therefore, pay careful attention to your thoughts and desires, and focus on what you desire with gratitude and appreciation. It's how the Law of Attraction works in your life.

Be mindful of the Law of Circulation, which demands continuous flow. If you choose to block that flow anywhere in the cycle, you stop your good. If you feel unworthy or undeserving, you will block the flow of the Law of Financial Circulation in your life.

If you feel uncomfortable about accepting a gift or even a compliment, the core problem is not money; it's your feeling of unworthiness.

Money, in and of itself, is neither good nor evil. Money is simply the commodity we currently use to acquire goods and services. Centuries ago, we were exchanging beads and seashells.

So, when did we begin to have an issue with money? For many of us, this fear of money began when we were children. I was terrified when I heard at Sunday School that money was evil and if I loved money, I wouldn't go to heaven. Yikes, I wanted to go to heaven! I was also frightened by monsters under my bed and noises outside my window.

As I grew, I realized the monsters weren't real, there was no such thing as the boogeyman, and if I hear scraping against the house, I know now it's time to trim the trees.

Yet, the concept that money was in and of itself as being evil lingered in the darkness recesses of my subconscious mind. It was compounded by the often-heard declarations from my parents that I was unworthy. Over time, the fear of money and the belief that I was unworthy to have money assimilated in my psyche.

This feeling, this fear, this negative energy grew roots and blocked my path to financial abundance for many years.

Gradually and over time, I realized I was a beloved child of God, worthy of every good thing. It took countless books, tapes, and CDs, as well as a lot of internal dialogue and hard work to eradicate my thoughts and feelings of unworthiness.

What are your thoughts of unworthiness? What are your thoughts about money? Do you feel awkward about accepting money? How do you feel about enjoying money?

Now I want you to look at the bigger picture and examine your feelings and worthiness of having a financially successful business practice.

If you feel in any way hesitant about accepting money, may I suggest you sit in a quiet spot, hold a dollar bill in your hand, close your eyes, and allow yourself to explore your thoughts and feelings about money.

Let the money talk to you. Listen to what it says and how your body reacts to this internal dialogue. See yourself receiving money; as you receive your payment, what does your body tell you? Does your sacral chakra constrict? Is there a lump in your throat or a knot in your stomach?

I want you to visualize yourself paying a bill. Do you write your check out with joy and gratitude for the service you received, or are you fearful as you watch your balance grow smaller? Identify all physical and emotional experiences as you spend your money. Your body is a barometer of your intuitive self. The sheer act of identifying negative thoughts and emotions will help you root them out.

To break any fear or money blockage in your life, give. Give, give, give! Giving stimulates the Law of Circulation and galvanizes the Universe to create a fresh financial flow into your life.

The next time you go into a restaurant or write a check, take a moment to experience the energy flow that goes out from you during this transaction. If any restrictions occur, identify and release them until there is nothing left but gratitude for the meal you enjoyed. Practice this activity until you feel delight for the experience and the deep-seated knowingness that the money you just gave is now in circulation will return to you.

As you pay for your meal, see that money flowing from you to the server, to the restaurant owner, and to the farmer who buys and plants the seed. Feel the happiness of each exchange and the joy in each interaction by every person in the monetary chain. Watch your money moves to the bankers and businesses and to all the people who enjoy the happy benefit you set into motion. Feel the happiness of the employees who are able to make their house payment or buy toys for their children and food for their tables. The money, freely and lovingly given, will return to you, multiplied.

Learn to give and accept money with gratitude. Let go of any negative thoughts you have about money. Replace those thoughts with an attitude of gratitude by happily and joyfully accepting the funds, funds you are worthy to accept and experience.

Practice the act of gracious receiving. Be open to receiving money and learn how to say thank you as you receive. To say anything other than thank you is to dishonor the giver. Thank the giver, thank God, and bless the funds.

I have noticed that people who have difficulty accepting money also have difficulty accepting a compliment. If you feel a lump in your throat when someone says something nice about your dress or your person, don't dismiss their compliment by disrespecting their opinion. Simply say thank you and nothing more. Practice saying thank you until you can accept a compliment with gratitude. Compliments and money go hand in hand in the heart.

Money needs to be kept in a constant state of flow. It's okay to add to your savings or hold onto it for a prosperous future; just don't hold onto it out of the fear that if you spend it, it won't return.

Live in the Laws of Attraction and Circulation, and money, love, and abundance will flow continuously in your life.

Say with me and know in your heart of hearts, "I now accept love, health, harmony, and financial abundance in my life. I enjoy the flow of financial abundance in my life. I give generously and I pay my bills, knowing money is continuously flowing into my life. I am worthy of every good thing. I am worthy of an unending stream of financial abundance. And So It Is."

CHAPTER 4

WHEN AFFIRMATIONS DON'T WORK

An affirmation is a proclamation, a truth you claim, to affect your life. When you speak an affirmation, you speak the here and now that is soon to be. Positive affirmations can shift consciousness to bring about a positive change in the physical world.

However, merely repeating a phrase or affirmation over and over again without investing your personal energy behind the words is merely wishful thinking.

I want you to liken your affirmation to a jet airplane. Picture a beautiful, gleaming airplane sitting on the tarmac. You're in the captain's chair, but until you engage the engines, the jet is going to sit idling on the runway. By physically pushing the throttle forward, the engines roar to life and drive the plane forward before the airplane ascends into powder-blue sky. The energy, your energy behind your words, will give your affirmations flight.

The first step is to believe your words and then put energy into them. Belief combined with your emotions and energy are the wind beneath your wings.

Most of us at one time or another have dieted. You began each day resolute in your determination to stick to your healthy eating plan; that is until a coworker brings donuts to the office. Your intellect reminds you that donuts are not on your food plan, yet the heady aromatic scent of warm pastry triggers your taste buds and reminds you of the savory sweetness of the soft, cream-filled treats. Your desire to enjoy the donut overrides your willpower. When the emotions and the intellect come in conflict, the emotions will always win. I'm going to add here, dieters, you can win this battle by replacing fleeting emotions with more powerful, positive desire. Your emotional energy will follow the stronger emotional call.

Christ stated in Matthew 18:19, "Again I say unto you, that if two of you shall agree on earth as touching anything that they shall ask, it shall be done for them of my Father which is in heaven." The two or more this verse is addressing is the intellect and emotion; these are the two that must come together and agree before manifestation occurs.

Affirmations don't work because the Universe responds to what we focus our attention. Thoughts are things. What you think about and dwell on, you will experience in the manifest plane. The Universe is always listening to your inner thoughts and your emotional energy and will respond accordingly. In fact, not only will the Universe respond but what you give your attention to will come back to you multiplied.

Years ago, I would spend the first thirty minutes of each morning in prayer and meditation as I spiritually built my financial wealth. During my prayers and meditation, I truly sparked the Divine within me and I was one with my good. Oh, if only I could have stayed there!

You see, immediately after my morning meditations, I would check my bank balance and then spend the next twenty-three-plus hours worrying about money and what I perceived as my lack of it.

I set into play the Universal Laws of Attraction and Correspondence which returned to me as an unending cycle of financial challenges.

Whatever we send out, comes back multiplied.

As I grew in faith, I stopped that cycle by turning my attention and completely focusing on abundance throughout the day. As I directed my attention and my thoughts to prosperity, the Universe opened the floodgates of financial increase.

What are you focusing your attention on throughout the day?

I heard one of my favorite stories at a Christian Science Lecture. My apologies to the speaker, whose name has become lost in time, but the picture he painted still resonates with me today.

He shared a story of an old lady who barely had enough to eat. Her children had deserted her, her husband had left her for another woman, and her home was falling around her. Lamenting her life, she went to her minister for solace.

"What have you asked God for?" the minister asked gently.

With tears in her eyes, she said in a voice barely above a whisper, "All I have ever asked God for was crust of bread and a roof over my head."

The moral of this tale seems harsh, but the lesson is clear: each of us gets exactly what we ask for. Therefore, take care and examine what you are asking of Heaven.

Another favorite story of mine is of an Irish lad who measured out a few loaves of bread and cheese for his long voyage across the Atlantic to America. He kept a close eye on his rations he had brought with him. As the days passed, the bread, he brought with him, grew moldy, and the cheese went bad. Day after day, he listened to the happy mealtimes shared by the other passengers. It wasn't until they neared the shore did, he come to understand that his ticket included the generous meals served daily. Your "ticket" to this life includes abundant.

In John 10:10, Jesus states, "I am come that they might have life, and that they might have it more abundantly."

Too often, we limit ourselves with false and self-limiting thoughts. How many of us ask for little when the Universe is willing to give us so much more, if only we'd accept it? You were born to be successful. You were born success filled. It's your nature.

If you are struggling to find that abundance in your life, start by counting your blessings. Every morning, every night, thank God for your good. As your list grows with an attitude of gratitude, so will your financial circumstances.

Rise above fear and doubt, through the knowingness that your affirmations and your words are true for you. Energize those affirmations with the confidence found in your emotions.

When working with my clients, I will often prescribe an affirmation, just as physicians give patients a prescription. Instead of two pills a day, I'd suggest they repeat an affirmation every hour on the hour.

"I am a successful. I am success filled. I have an abundance of clients who are grateful for my service. I thank the Universe for my customers and clients. With gratitude, I welcome and receive financial abundance for my work for the benefit of all."

Think only thoughts of success. Speak only words of success.

At a prosperity seminar, I once heard the speaker share that she would go to the mall, walk through the stores, all the while looking at all the beautiful clothes, jewelry, and accessories. When the clerks asked if they could help her, she'd always respond, "No thank you, I'm just manifesting." How cool is that! Today, her closets are filled with designer clothes, and her jewelry box is overflowing with diamonds and pearls.

Another reason why affirmations don't work is due to outlining. Outlining is telling God exactly what must take place and in what exact order. This is called outlining. The Universe might have greater plans for you. Telling the Universe exactly how it is to happen might block your ultimate good. One of my clients wanted a new car. She came to me with an outline of how this was to occur. Her plan began with a visit a car dealership, test-driving the vehicle, and being offered payments she could afford, well, barely afford. Instead of outlining each detail of how the plan should unfold, I recommended she start with the answer, which was a car. After a few weeks of visualizing her car, repeating her affirmations, and releasing her request to the Universe, she received a call from her aunt. Her aunt wanted to gift her with the exact car she had held in her visualization. Don't outline; visualize your desired outcome. Start with the answer.

Sometimes those searching for love, some New Agers enjoy creating an enormous treasure map, filled with beautiful pictures of how and where to meet Mr. or Ms. Right, followed by a fairytale romance, with the outcome a lovely wedding. Treasure mapping can be fun, but take care about being too specific. Pasting Brad Pitt's picture on a treasure map is okay if you understand the picture is but a representation of what you desire. Telling the Universe to give you Brad Pitt might not work, as the Universe may have other plans for the handsome Mr. Pitt and you.

I always, always recommend adding the phrase to any prayer or affirmation, "This or something better now manifests for me." This allows the Universe to give you something more than you can imagine for yourself.

Some people like to say their affirmations before a mirror. If this works for you, by all means, do it. I write my affirmations and repeat them throughout each day. Do what works for you.

Say your affirmation with belief, conviction, and focus on the outcome of your desire.

If you put positive energy behind your affirmations and then release them to the Universe in peace and confidence, I assure you, the Universe will respond.

CHAPTER 5

CORD CUTTING

On occasion, there seems to be something elusive holding us back from our success. It's not quite tangible, but you know it's there. Some will dismiss the feeling by proclaiming that Mercury in is retrograde. As metaphysicians, we know to look deeper so we can take corrective measures and steady our course. We may not be cognizant of the cause, but we know we are experiencing the effect. The causation eludes us.

If this is the case, it may be a lingering Etherical Cord that is binding us to a forgotten experience in our current life or perhaps a past life.

I see etherical cords as thin, fine, shimmering, silvery, magical tubing that glitters and sparkles between us and those we love. While most cannot see these etherical cords, we can feel them binding us to those we love and those who love us. We can feel them tug at us, when we sense a loved one is in distress or even danger.

These cords also bind us to experiences, places, and things.

Etherical cords connect us not only to loved ones but to strangers with whom we feel an instant connection. We are so immediately familiar with these strangers; it seems as if we have known them all our lives. With these new friends there is never a moment of awkwardness, and even the silence seems natural.

The French term déjà vu which means "already seen." Etherical Cords are déjà vu experiences that are felt.

Etherical Cords can bind us to painful experiences, hurtful relationships, and traumatic events. Like soldiers with PTSD, an intrusive sound can flash us back to those painful memories, and those memories can be from our current life or centuries past.

Have you ever met anyone who is inherently afraid of water, fire, or heights, with no experience in this lifetime to base it on? These fears and frightening memories may not have come from a childhood event but from another life that was lived centuries ago.

I may very well be the only person in America who becomes unnerved at the sight of a Viking longboat. It's okay to laugh, I do but I also have a clear and distinct memory of Vikings attacking an abbey where I lived during the twelfth century. I endured a horrific death in that lifetime and was still tied to it by an etherical cord. I became aware of this fear one evening while watching a television show. At the first glimpse of a Viking ship sailing on a river in Northern Ireland, my body shook in panic, my throat went dry, and my body was stricken in fear. I was unnerved for hours without understanding why the image frightened me so. A few days later, in a past-life regression, I saw my death on the steps of a monastery. I understood why the image was so terrifying to me, and I was able to release the fear and cut the etherical cord that bound me to it.

Sometimes the frightening visions you conjure in your dreams are not nightmares or a product of your imagination; they are memories. Whether in this lifetime or a previous lifetime, we may hold on to a buried memories or experiences that are so deep, we can no longer recall the trauma, but the etherical cord remains until we release these harrowing events.

Once when I was working with a beautiful young woman, I could sense there was a past relationship that was holding her back from experiencing the love which she now longed for. I could sense she was still bound by the strong etherical cord she had created between her abusive lover and the memories she held of him.

"Do you think of that him more than three times a week?" I asked, already anticipating her answer.

She laughed. "I think of him three times an hour."

She was tied to a relationship that had ended years ago. The painful relationship was keeping her from experiencing a loving relationship she now craved.

By identifying this unhealthy cord, we began working on cutting this unhealthy fetter. It took several cord cuttings to completely sever this particular tie. While we worked on this, she also learned to reprogram her energy to attract a loving partner who would treat her with love and respect. It took several weeks to completely cut her attachment, but in the end, she was successful. As if on cue, a man who seemed to be everything she had dreamed about came into her life. Today, she is living her happily ever after with her new husband, who treasures her and supports her every dream.

Some Etherical Cords are not so easily identifiable. For instance, we may have spoken vows of poverty in a past life where we were monks, priests, or in a holy order where we swore such oaths. I strongly posture that as you now align yourself in service to others, you may have had a life as a healer or served in a religious order where you swore such a vow. I made such a vow of poverty in the eleventh century and brought it forward with me to this lifetime.

If any of these words or experiences resonate within you, there may be a cord that needs to be cut. You don't need to remember the moment you made such a vow; it's simply enough to know it's there. I assure you God does not want you to live in poverty.

The act of cutting a cord does not have to be a complicated ceremony, in fact it's very simple. I work with Archangels, so when I need to cord cut, I call on Archangel Michael and ask him to use his fiery sword to sever my ties to any person, place, or thing that does not serve me. After a cord cutting, I always ask Archangel Raphael to salve the wound with his green healing light to complete the healing.

For some etherical cords, a single cord cutting will do. Other cords are strong and will regrow. If this is the case, be aware that some cords need to be cut several times before they completely dissipate. Continue to cut those cords until you are no longer bound to people or painful memories that haunt you. They have no place in your current life. There are many different methods for cord cutting. Find one that feels right and natural to you.

If you feel you need to contact a professional, there are wonderful metaphysical practitioners who can assist you in cord cutting on the internet. Keep the loving, beautiful cords that bind you to loving relationships, but cut any cords that keep you from experiencing your good.

CHAPTER 6

PROCRASTINATION

Ask any writer of my generation, and they will tell you the longest distance in the world is from the easy chair to the typewriter—or now it's to computer. I can vouch for this, as some days I will seek out the most unnecessary chores to delay my journey to my work in progress.

Delaying work on a project is not the exclusive domain of authors; procrastination has evolved into an American pastime. Everyone procrastinates at one time or another. Postponing a task for hours or even days suggests there may be a deeper issue to holding you back from your success.

There are many reasons for procrastination. One of the reasons we postpone projects is because the task appears to be too monumental. I'd run screaming from my home if I thought I had to create a three-hundred-page novel in a single setting. Instead, I break down the book into comfortable pieces. My daily goal is to write three to five pages a day. This results in one chapter a week. By breaking down the process into a manageable size, I can complete a book in six months.

If you find yourself procrastinating, take a moment and understand what is keeping you from completing your project. If it seems overwhelming, break it down into smaller tasks. Smaller tasks will make your project more manageable.

If you are postponing a chore because you do not know how to execute an undertaking, then your job is not to struggle with the task but to learn how to undertake it. For example, if you need to write a press release but are postponing it because you don't know how to format a press release, your task is not writing the actual press release but learning how to format and structure a great press release.

Eliminate minor distractions that cause you to procrastinate. For example, do the dishes the night before. Narrow your route to your work projects by clearing your schedule so that nothing will impede your journey the next morning. Set your intentions for the next day the night before.

Identify and break habits that no longer serve you. Commit to a daily schedule. Establish your business's start time, and adhere to that schedule. Do this for twenty-one days, and on day twenty-one, if not before, you will have created a new pattern or routine in your life.

Another favorite trick of mine is to set a kitchen timer for twenty minutes. After all, anyone can commit to a twenty-minute time period, right? Don't be surprised to find yourself working long after your timer has stopped ringing.

While on this topic, if you enjoy all those cute animal videos as I do, and if you need to take a break during your day, set that timer for twenty minutes to refresh your spirit, and then get back to your business!

Be a goal-setter. At the end of your work week, make it a habit to write down your tasks and goals for the coming week. At the end of the day, create a to-do list for the next day. I find there is something very satisfying about crossing off items from your list.

An associate of mine hated making phone calls, Phone calls, however, were a necessity for her business. For her to accomplish this goal, she had to commit to making thirty phone calls a day. As she made each call, she would drop a shiny new penny into a crystal goblet. Each cheerful little cling of the copper pennies resonated throughout her office. This delightful audio clue represented income for her family and success in her business. She went from loathing the task to looking forward to completing her calls each day.

If you find yourself procrastinating, find a solution to complete each necessary task.

Do what you need to do each day and remember you are the one who makes your magic happen.

CHAPTER 7

THE BRIDE'S PRICE

Centuries ago, a young American Indian male would offer war ponies in exchange for a bride. This exchange was known as the Bride's Price, and in some cultures, it's still practiced today.

Any goal worth achieving comes with a price. If your goal is a physically fit body, you make time to exercise. The media is filled with stories of a lone athlete rising before dawn, logging long, countless miles before receiving Olympic gold.

Today, entrepreneurs pay the Bride's Price by investing in themselves with time, money, and effort. What is the price you need to pay to make your practice a success? Unless you have the luxury of having all the funds you need to start your new practice, you may, at least initially, have to set aside a set number of hours a day or week to plan, create, or start your own your spiritual practice. This takes commitment, but this is important to you and your successful practice. This may mean forgoing lunch with friends or turning off your favorite television shows.

I would love to have a Fairy Godmother who would wave her magic wand and bring my novels to life. In the real world, I'm the one who has to make time, do research, and put in the hours necessary to complete each novel. For years, this meant getting up at 4:00 a.m. to spend two hours working on my novel before waking my family for breakfast.

Starting your own full-time or part-time business may mean arriving early, working through lunch, or working late into the night to get your spiritual practice off the ground. Setting time for your marketing and public-relations campaigns, which will make your practice a success, will require the time investment of arriving early or dedicating a specific amount to time to work on your marketing initiatives.

I want to assure you there is a light at the end of the tunnel; once you are established, the demands on your time will lessen, and you will have the time to enjoy the fruits of your labor. In the meantime, in the startup phase of your practice, you may have to pay the Bride's Price to make your magic happen.

As you make your practice a priority, don't forget to create a balance in your life. Make time for your children, family, and friends, as they are your support team, and you don't want to crowd them out.

You are in charge of your success. You have already made the decision to stop working for someone else and invest in time and money in yourself. I'm in your front row cheering. The tools in this book are designed to help you become a success.

Each moment of every day is going to be a choice, your choice, your commitment to your dream. Pay the Bride's Price for success, because you are so worth it!

CHAPTER 8

SABOTEURS

You can find saboteurs at work, among your circle of friends, your family, and in the mirror. The mission of a saboteur is to obstruct your journey and to keep you from reaching your highest good.

Many times, saboteurs are not consciously aware of their crippling influence on your life. They may harbor the belief that if you become too successful, too rich, or too thin, you may no longer need them in your life. Their rationale may make perfect sense to them, but it damages you.

My Dad was one of those people. In 1967, he told me I would never be anything but a hash slinger. Note, there nothing at all wrong with being a server, none whatsoever, but in his world, this was his way of telling me I would never amount to anything, certainly not achieve my dreams as a writer. Far worse than his harsh words were the fact that I believed them. My self-esteem plummeted, and for decades, his appalling words became so entrenched in my psyche, they grew and spilled into every area of my life. Many years later, he apologized to me. I had already forgiven him, but it took me years of counseling until I was able to rise above the pain. My father was one of my first saboteurs, unfortunately, he was not my last.

Once in a toxic relationship, I had set upon a goal of weight loss. My saboteur brought home pizza on Friday nights and donuts to my office in the mornings. While my coworkers gushed at how thoughtful he was, I cried when I saw his "gifts". I cried as I ate them, and I hated myself after eating them.

I did not understand why he could not support me on my weight-loss journey. He never explained his motives, but as time passed, I came to understand his agenda; you see, if I stayed fat, no one would want me. If no one wanted me, I would stay with him and put up with his lying and cheating ways. Thankfully, I saw him for what he was and got rid of him and the weight.

Today, some of our saboteurs are assigned cute little names and identified as frenemies. Frienemies have their own reasons to keep you from reaching your goals. Some frenemies encouraged me to go out for drinks or indulge in desserts, telling me I deserved to treat myself. Others saddled me with their negative emotions, and I allowed myself to become a dumping ground for their problems. As an empath, I absorbed their negative emotions, and once they had unburdened their emotional baggage on me, my friends would be light as a feather while I carried their burden for days.

I had to cut these emotional saboteurs from my life. Don't worry, they moved on and attached themselves to other people who would be open to their emotional neediness. Those who I could help, I did. The others I had to leave along the path to complete their own journeys.

I also had to put my dreams ahead of being an entertaining sidekick. Friends are fun and certainly play an important part of your life, but so are your dreams. Find a balance for both.

The award for worst saboteur goes to myself. I needed no outside influences to sabotage my dreams. I was an unending source of self-sabotaging behavior. It took time to overcome my own self-sabotaging, but I did slowly climb out of the mire of unworthiness and voices of self-doubt. It can be hard to drown out negative voices, but it can be done. Believe in yourself, and remember, real friends will support your dreams. Those who truly love and support you will be in your front row, cheering.

James Van Praagh has a wonderful class called "The Highly Sensitives Survival Guide". If you are an empath like me, I urge you to take his class. All of James Van Praagh's classes are wonderful and life-changing. You can find these classes at James Van Praagh's School of Mystical Arts.

When dealing with saboteurs, allow the Universe and the Angels help you see the truth of your soul's experience.

Don't let anyone, even yourself, keep you from your success. Surround yourself with positive people, positive thoughts, and positive messages.

To lift my spirit on track, I purchased a small notebook and filled it with positive affirmations. I made it a point to read them on the hour, every hour until I internalized them and came to believe and accept them as my truth.

If you need additional support, create your own support group. Members of your team can be real or imagined. Surround yourself with people and words that inspire you on your positive journey. You will find more information about setting up your own support team in Part IV of this book.

Saboteurs have no place in your business practice. Identify them, lift them up if you can, or release them if you must. Remember, you were touched by heaven to be successful. Believe in yourself and have faith. Become the hero or heroine of your adventure and know, I wrote this book for you because I believe in you and your dream!

CHAPTER 9

BUILDING CONFIDENCE

Confidence is the inner knowingness, the self-assurance that you know you can complete a task. Confidence is not boastful, nor does it make you feel superior to others. Confidence simply means you know how to complete a task.

I want you to reflect on areas of your life in which you do have confidence. For example, if you need groceries, you know how to drive your car to the store, make your food selections, pay for them, and then return home. After all, you say to yourself, "I have done this hundreds of times. Of course, I know how to accomplish this."

However, there was a time, however, when you didn't know how to drive an automobile or purchase groceries. You learned how to do both. There was a time when you didn't know how to walk or talk, and you learned.

Today, you are the master in all types of achievements and have the self-confidence to can accomplish each task with assured success.

Having your own business may be new to you, and you may feel a bit wobbly and unsure about achieving your success. Your lack of confidence in yourself and this lacks lack of confidence, may be keeping you at a nine-to-five job. Release any voice inside you that says you can't start your own spiritual practice.

To have confidence in fulfilling your dream, first be confident in your talent and abilities. Know that you know. Acquire confidence by reading books and articles on becoming an entrepreneur. Internalize their messages. Build your self-confidence by knowing you are an expert in your field of study.

Create a book of affirmations and reasons why you deserve to own your own practice, as well as why you will be a success at it. Repeat your affirmations every hour on the hour until you know them to be true. Think and act successful, and you will be.

In Part IV of this book, I am going to walk you through creating your own Business Plan and a Promotional Calendar. Writing your business plan and creating your promotional calendar will give you the confidence and know how you need to succeed.

Each morning and each night, visualize a successful spiritual practice. Read books on success. Read books on prosperity. As you read, practice, and visualize your own success, you will gradually still the voice of fear and build the knowingness that you can.

We all know the children's story of the little train engine that could. It was written in the 1930s, and it's still found on top one hundred children's book lists. It's successful because its message resonates within each of us.

Like the *Little Engine That Could*, we begin our journeys feeling a little unsure but optimistic as we begin the ascend. As we move forward, our optimism grows, bolstered by small successes. With each success, we continue to climb until we reach the top and we move from the consciousness of I think I can to knowing I could. That's confidence! One day, from the pinnacle of your successful spiritual practice, you will look back and say, "I knew I could, I knew I could!"

The more steps you take in starting your spiritual practice, the more confident you will be. If you know that you know, you will have the faith and ability in yourself and your dream, and you will have the confidence to create your own successful spiritual practice.

You will build, then reinforce your confidence as you follow the passion in your heart.

You will find your self-confidence inside of you. Self-confidence is the inner knowing and the self-assurance that you deserve to be a success and that you are success filled and successful.

You see, everything you need is already inside you.

CHAPTER 10

MANIFESTATION THROUGH VISUALIZATION

Visualization is the technique of creating a visual image in the mind. Daydreams are not targeted visualizations. Daydreams will sometimes work if we put enough energy behind them, but as a whole, allowing your mind to simply drift with no real direction will not bring a fanciful thought into the manifest plane. Visualization will convert your images into reality.

I believe the underlying foundation of the Law of Attraction is visualization, for as we visualize, we breathe life into our thoughts. You give life to your desire by infusing it with emotional energy. You can change your life through visualization, and you can certainly affect your spiritual practice.

We have heard a thousand times that thoughts are things. What we think or dwell on comes into our experience. By adding visualizations into your success-filled thoughts, you fuel your energy and more closely and accurately secure your outcome.

The whimsical thought of owning a new car is not going to put you in the driver's seat. By activating the Law of Attraction and focusing your attention to how it will feel to drive that car, how the new car will smell, how it will take a turn, and the pleasure you will feel driving it, will bring it into the manifest plane.

When the subconscious mind and energy combine, they will bring forth your desire. This is the two or more stated in the Bible; the two being the mind or intellect and the heart or emotion.

The subconscious mind will accept your desired visualization as real, and this is how thoughts become things and through the Law of Attraction, that which you desire is made manifest into your experience.

The trifecta of the Law of Attraction is stating your intention, deeply feeling your success, and then releasing it to the Universe. Visualize your desire in detail. If you are a yoga instructor, see your customers entering your studio and completing a full workout. Notice in your mind's eye what everyone is wearing, the color of their mats, the flow of their arms and bodies as they move from pose to pose. In your visualized imagery, hear the music and listen to yourself giving instructions. Fully embrace the experience and feel the gratitude of your customers thanking you for a beautiful practice as they happily pay for their class.

If you are a Medium, visualize customers being drawn to you from the four corners of the globe. Ask the Angels to help guide people to your practice and know, truly know, the right customers will come to you through your marketing efforts. See them scheduling appointments and prepaying for their sessions. See your appointment book filled with clients. In your mind's eye and ear, watch as you see yourself soothing their hearts with divine communications. See them with immense gratitude thanking you for your class and enjoy the deep satisfaction of a job well done.

If you have a New Age store, visualize people coming into the store, examining items, making purchases, asking you questions, attending your events, and signing up for readings and being grateful for your services and for the items they purchase.

As you see and feel your practice as successful, also see your customers happily paying you for your services. Visualize the money flowing from your customers' hands, checkbooks, and credit cards into your bank account. See yourself happily accepting it and thanking your customers.

As the money floods into your account, see yourself paying your mortgage, your electric bill, enjoying lunch with friends, and whatever expenditure that pleases you. Visualize your imagery in vibrant colors and always say the words, "This or something more now manifests for me."

As you move through the chapters of this book, take time to visualize and capture each marketing strategy and see it successful.

Used effectively, with stated intention, visualizations combined with faith will turn your visualization into reality. And so, it is!

Visualization Guide

1. Have a clear picture in your mind of your Desire.
2. Write your Intention with Energy behind each word.
3. Prepare yourself by Grounding, Meditation, and Connecting to the Universe
4. Visualize your Desired Outcome by putting Energy, Passion, and Feeling into your Imagery.
5. Infuse Love and Detail into every aspect of your Visualization.
6. End your Visualization with an overwhelming sense of Gratitude!
7. Release your Desire to the Universe
8. Create a Faith that knows your desire Will manifest.
9. Throughout the day, connect to your Visualization through act, in word and deed, with a dedicated knowingness your Desire is already true.
10. Create an affirmation and say your affirmation every hour on the hour.
11. Live as though your Vision is true, always add, this or something better now manifests in my life.
12. End with your Visualization by saying, Amen or And So, It is!"

CHAPTER 11

CONCLUSION: BUILDING THE FOUNDATION

As a Project Wild Educator, I have a collection of environmental educational games I play with children. One of my favorite games is a game. I begin by cupping a small acorn in my hand, and I ask my young audience to guess what I was holding.

"How tall is it?" they ask. I peek, careful to keep the acorn hidden in my palm. I reply, "It looks to be about eighty feet tall." I watch their eyes widen. "What color is it? How big is it?" The questions continued until they can think of no more to ask. Only then I slowly reveal the little acorn in my hand. The children scream with delight. I continue.

"You see," I'd explain, "everything this little acorn needs, is already inside of it. Its nature is to grow over eighty feet. One day it will provide homes for birds and squirrels as well as shelter for forest animals." I continue to explain and tell the children before me that like the acorn, every child already has everything they each need to grow and thrive inside of each of them.

You have everything you need for your success; it's already inside you.

As you read through the following chapters, you will begin to understand how to develop a Marketing Plan for your spiritual practice.

In Part II, you will find information on real-world marketing, promotional opportunities, and public relations. In Part III, you will find ways to promote your business online. Part IV will help you put your thoughts and ideas into a solid business plan and an annual promotional calendar.

Give your dreams love, plant your spiritual practice in fertile soil, and remove doubts and all negative thinking that are holding you back. Make your foundation strong.

God gave you your gifts to help others. You truly are a blessing to this world. God, the Universe would never give you a dream without also giving you the fulfillment of that desire.

Every day, I urge you to meditate, to connect with the Universe and elevate your consciousness. Every day, I urge you to spend time in meditation and visualization. Bless your spiritual practice, and whether you begin your business at a brick-and-mortar store or at the kitchen table, you are now standing on holy ground.

You were born to succeed; it's your birthright.

PART II

REAL WORLD ADVERTISING, MARKETING, AND PUBLIC RELATIONS

CHAPTER 12

OVERVIEW: MARKETING, ADVERTISING, AND PUBLIC RELATIONS

As you begin this section, I'd like to recommend you keep a notebook handy to jot down your thoughts and marketing strategies you find appealing and plan to incorporate into your marketing plans. You don't have to fulfill every initiative outlined in this book, but I do suggest you keep notes on marketing strategies that appeal to you and could fit into your life and your budget.

By keeping a record of your thoughts, you'll have a clearer vision of what you want to incorporate into your Business Plan and Promotional Calendar when you reach the final section of this book.

Let's begin by understanding the differences and similarities between marketing, advertising, and public relations.

Marketing is the term that encompasses the entire spectrum of advertising, public relations, publicity, and promotions. Under the marketing umbrella, you will set goals, create strategies, establish budgetary parameters, and forecast financial projections.

Advertising is paid messages in which you attempt to attract and influence consumers to buy your product or services. You pay for advertising. Examples of paid advertisements are ads featured in newspapers or magazines, as well as television, radio commercials, and billboards.

A cost-effective way to capture attention is through public relations, promotions, and publicity. Unlike paid advertising, publicity and public relations, for the most part, are free. You will be responsible for the creation of your publicity, which may require using an advertising agency, graphic designer, or freelance copywriter. You can, of course, reduce the costs by doing it yourself. A strong publicity campaign will give you credibility, name recognition, and will help you build and solidify your brand.

The next chapter will deep dive into understanding what Branding is and why it is important to you.

CHAPTER 13

BRANDING

Branding is the marketing term that identifies you, your products and services. No matter how big or how small your practice is, branding is important to you.

Your Brand will differentiate you from your competitors, and properly executed, your brand will build trust and loyalty. Brand images and messages improve recognition and trust. A well-established Brand will help you achieve your goals.

Branding incorporates your name, your logo, tag lines, colors, and fonts, and even the sounds associated with a distinct brand. Yes, sounds.

For example, the signature "dun, dun" sound of *Law and Order* is recognizable and heralds the start of one of America's favorite television crime dramas.

Branding began at the turn of the twentieth century but didn't fully come of age until the introduction of radio. As marketeers began to understand the reach and power of radio to influence consumers. Advertisements moved from radio to television and into all advertising mediums.

A classic example of Branding is Kleenex. Kleenex is the name of the company that produces tissues, but the name has become so synonymous with the product that we often ask for a Kleenex instead of a tissue.

Formulating your Brand takes a lot of thought and attention. Like a happy marriage, you want to get it right the first time, as you will be living with your choices a long time.

To create your Brand, you must first know who you are and have a clear understanding of your market and your demographics. Demographics define the makeup of an area's population. Demographics include age, gender, education, interests, and income. Segments of the population can be further refined and broken down further. Your goal is to understand what segments of your area's population would be most likely purchase your products and services. This is your demographics group, which I will be referring to as your target market.

As you contemplate your brand, uncover what makes you unique and different from others in your field. Understanding who you are and the services you offer will connect you to your customers, your demographic group. Study at your competition, not to appropriate their images or messages but to learn how you can set yourself apart from them.

For many years, the advertising agency I worked for would market hotels and resorts that literally stood next door to one another. Same market, same demographics. We were able to acquire these accounts by understanding how each hotel was distinctive from the other and then focus on the hotel's uniqueness in the marketplace.

Another example would be of fast-food chains that are located beside one another. Both restaurants sell hamburgers, fries, and shakes, but each has its own unique brand and message. Their respective messages appeal to specific market segments. Customers respond to the advertising messages and support the brand that resonates most with them.

Branding can take time and thought. Even the pros, like myself, will tell you this is not an overnight process.

If you still want to explore branding further, the next time you visit the grocery store, consider any product on the shelves. For instance, there seem to be hundreds of cans and jars of spaghetti sauce. Each company offers different packaging and branding, but all basically follow the same formula of tomato and spices with slight variations. Their brand and the brand messaging shape your decision as to which one you will purchase.

As you contemplate your brand, make a list of words and phrases that would best describe your practice. Keep refining your thoughts until you come up with three to seven words that best communicate what your spiritual practice is about. The most powerful brand is one that emotionally connects to your customers.

A picture is worth a thousand words, therefore, selecting the right image for your logo will help your customers understand and connect to you.

Bring your brand to life with colors. Think of colors most associated with your industry. Once you select your colors and the fonts you will use, you will want to incorporate these into your website, your business cards, and signage. The colors and fonts become part of brand and shape the unique look you want to project to the world.

Your brand is the sum of who you are, your message, your logo, and identity all neatly bundled in an attractive package designed to attract customers to your spiritual practice.

As your company evolves over time, you may choose to modify your brand's identity. It's important to build a strong foundation first.

Years ago, my brand, my logo was my name with a strong image of beautiful red lips and a smoking gun. A viewer's takeaway from my logo would be I write romantic suspense. As I now have evolved to multiple genres to include marketing, I changed my brand and logo and carried the new look to my blog site, *TheBusinessSide.blog*.

Every now and then, the magic happens; but for most of us, branding takes time, but it is so worth the effort. As your brand becomes synonymous with your practice, you become the standard by which all others in your industry are judged.

In the next several chapters, we will continue to look more at more elements that fuse into what is your Brand.

CHAPTER 14

THE HIGH CONCEPT AND ELEVATOR PITCH

A High Concept and Elevator Pitch are a very important part of your Branding. These two important components have endless uses and ongoing applications across social media and in real-world marketing initiatives. The High Concept and Elevator Pitch are your marketing's launch pad to financial success.

The High Concept

The high concept is a catchphrase designed to explain your business in a few words. Your high concept is a tagline that tells customers more about you.

The term High Concept was originated by book publishers' representatives who, when presenting a book to bookstore manager or buyer and had to quickly explain a novel. Today, the High Concept has evolved to describe movies, television shows, and businesses.

For example, to explain the movie *Jurassic Park,* marketers would say, "A theme park filled with dinosaurs. When security is breached, the dinosaurs escape." With this High Concept, you quickly understand this to be an exciting movie about dinosaurs and the terrifying consequences of dinosaurs unleashed on a modern world.

A couple of years ago, I was at the booksellers' convention, and I was standing behind a nice lady who was trying to tell two national radio show hosts about her book and why she should be on their show.

The author was very excited about her novel. I listened to her as she wandered about the storyline, pausing to describe various scenes and characters. She was clearly in love with the book's hero and heroine and how they fell in love. The Radio hosts listened politely. I watched as their eyes glazed over because they couldn't follow her long, rambling description.

I followed this lady, whose book was probably every bit as good as mine, but I gave the radio hosts my High Concepts. In a matter of moments, I clearly described my novels.

"My book *Lights, Camera, Murder!*" I began, "is a reality show that needs a real CSI. My second book is titled *Pirates in Paradise* is *Miami Vice* on a romantic *Midnight Run*. My romantic comedy *Your Cheatin' Hearts* is a Lucille Ball Comedy with a twist of *Magnum P.I.,* where pretty PI Shelby MacGregor always gets her man."

In a few short words, the radio hosts quickly understood what my books were about and asked me to appear on their show.

Creating your own High Concept will help explain your spiritual practice quickly and allows the recipient to quickly understand what you do and how your services will benefit them.

To develop your own High Concept, think about the amount of words on a billboard, seven words or less. Your High Concept should describe who you are and what your do in a quick, easy way. In this instance, it is okay to draw on popular movies, television shows, or pop culture icons.

Your High Concept can also be used on bookmarks, your website, and throughout your marketing strategies, including your email's signature line.

To create your own High Concept, I suggest you write a descriptive paragraph about your practice, then continue to break it down, consolidating sentences until you have a five- to seven-word description of your practice. Have fun developing yours.

Your High Concept is the first step toward solidifying your brand. It's who you are. It's what you are about, and when sharing your High Concept with others, will prompt interest in your spiritual practice. Your High Concept will easily fold into your tagline and support your marketing initiatives. Your High Concept will also play a key role in your elevator pitch.

The Elevator Pitch

An elevator pitch is a short introduction about your practice in which you describe your practice in thirty seconds or less to a potential client. The term Elevator Pitch is drawn from the average duration of a short elevator ride.

Your elevator pitch can also be incorporated into any type of introduction, from a one-on-one introduction or when being presented to hundreds of people. Below are a few examples.

Medium: "Hi, my name is Susie Q. I am a medium like James Van Praagh or the Long Island Medium. As a medium, I bridge the gap between loved ones who have passed on and those left behind."

Angel Card Reader or Angelic Life Coach: "Hi, my name is Susie Q. I am an Angel Card Reader. I help people connect with angels for advice on love, career, and life."

Yoga Instructor: "Hi, my name is Susie Q. I am a yoga instructor. I help people experience better health and sleep through yoga."

Your Elevator Pitch should be upbeat. After your introduction, pause for questions. Engage in a conversation and close your exchange by sharing a business or networking card.

For such occasions, when meeting people for the first time, I recommend you have several business or networking cards with special discounted offers. Be sure you keep discount cards separate from your regular business cards, as you don't want to offer discounts to everyone.

The purpose of the elevator pitch is to introduce your practice to potential customers and leave them wanting more. Practice your elevator pitch until you can recite it with enthusiasm and pride. You will be able to introduce yourself with confidence and make your practice memorable to everyone you meet.

CHAPTER 15

ADVERTISING

Advertising is the medium through which we promote our products, services, and goods. Advertisements cost money, whereas publicity and public relations campaigns are free, for the most part. Paid advertisements are guaranteed placement in media. There is no such guarantee with publicity.

Today, we are bombarded with advertising messages. In fact, statistics show the average person will be subject to around five thousand advertising messages a day.

Advertising messages stare at us from the back of cereal boxes and inside elevators and bathroom stalls. We see them on billboards, business signs, and billowing flag banners in front of car dealerships; hear them on the radio and see them on television. They appear in our emails and before the start of YouTube videos.

If you do decide to pay for your advertisements, make them count by target marketing into your demographic group.

Years ago, when cable was in its infancy, our advertising agency acquired a cable company that was on the verge of closing their business. The previous agency had placed the company's advertising dollars everywhere, causing a tremendous amount of wasteful spending and ineffective circulation. Their efforts did not result in sales. When the firm I worked for took over the client, we stopped this costly, wasteful spending and target marketed to the client's demographics, people who watched television. We reduced the customer's budget more than half and focused on buying ads in the TV publications. We also purchased a very few billboards in select locations and within six months increased the client's revenue by 600 percent.

This is a perfect example of why it's important to understand your demographics and to target your advertising dollars to the market segments who are most likely to buy your product or service.

I have been an advocate for target marketing long before the concept became popular. I am a big fan of utilizing free public relations promotional opportunities. It's not only less costly but precisely reaches your demographic group.

If you decide to use advertising to reach your clients, be aware that every radio, television, or newspaper advertising sales executive will tell you their format offers you the best opportunity to reach your market. It's their job, and in most cases, they are also paid only by commission. Always keep in mind, if you reach too broad a market, you will experience a lot of waste circulation and squander your advertising dollars.

Years ago, I was recommending an AM radio station to a client who owned a jewelry store. A FM radio representative who had met with them the day before boasted how their FM station reached over 120 miles from their store's location. The store owner liked that data until I pointed out, the FM's station had a much younger market as well the countless number of high-end jewelry stores a potential buyer would have to pass before reaching my client's location. I pointed out that the AM station reached a more local geographic area, and the listeners were older with discretionary income. The higher income would enable the older market to purchase the jeweler's luxury items. The store owner understood the advantage of local marketing. By opting for an AM station—as AM radio stations' commercials typically cost less than ads on FM stations—they spent less money to reach their market. In some cases, advertising on a large FM station would make sense; in this case, it did not.

Another example of reaching too broad a market is your local newspaper. Your regional newspaper may millions of subscribers but the actual percentage of readers who may be interested in your new age product or service may be relatively small. Despite their millions of readers, your ad will become lost in such a broad platform as most of their readers won't notice your ad, throw the newspaper out before finding or reading it, or will not be interested in purchasing your product in the first place.

In contrast, if you purchase an advertisement in a new age publication, your ad will reach a more receptive audience and offer you greater return for your money.

If you are aware of New Age publications in your area, contact the publication and propose an article about you. Also, consider placing a small ad with them for several weeks to gauge response. A good place to test the waters would be in the classified section. Before placing a larger ad, contact current advertisers to evaluate the response they are receiving.

Before you begin to even consider an advertising campaign, know your budget, stick to it, and calculate the results you'll receive from each individual ad. This is called ROI, return on investment. For example, if you spend $100 for an ad, you should expect at the very least $110 to $150 or more in new customers. Good advertising is only good if it works and if you a get responses.

Television and radio may be too costly for a small new age business, but that said, if James Van Praagh or John Edwards are appearing on a Dr. Phil episode or local morning show, you might want to consider a ten-second or thirty-second ad on that specific show. Call the station and introduce yourself to a sales executive and ask them if they are aware of any celebrity segments relative to your practice. If so, in this scenario, an investment might be worthwhile.

While it's great fun and glamorous to see your business on television, if it yields little or no results, don't spend your annual marketing budget on one or two television ads!

Look for advertising initiatives that yield a strong return and support your exposure and branding efforts.

You may wish to consider placing an ad in local high school or sports team's program, but of course, make sure your spiritual practice will be well received before buying an advertisement in a school's sports or drama program.

One of the opportunities I missed was advertising my name on a mug at one of my favorite restaurants. I didn't know about this opportunity until the waitress served my coffee in a mug wrapped in the names of local businesses. This would have been ideal for my practice, and unfortunately, I missed it. The ad on the mug would have cost pennies, and my ROI would have been a wealth of exposure. I did reach out to the promotional house for future opportunities within my community.

Advertise to your target market. Advertise only if it makes *cents*.

You can check on most newspapers, magazines, radio, and television advertisers by reviewing their online media kits, which will show you their demographics to confirm they match your target market group.

There will be some advertising mediums that make sense for you, especially any event program books of which you are a participant. However, for the most part, I recommend putting your time, energy, and marketing dollars into publicity and public relations campaigns.

Do what works for within your budget and your vision.

CHAPTER 16

ARTICLES AND OPPORTUNITIES ONLINE AND IN PRINT

One of the smartest ways to gain publicity is to have an article about your spiritual practice featured in a local, regional, or national publication. Editors are always on the lookout for interesting articles about individuals and businesses in their area. Why not let their readership know about you?

When readers read a well-written, positive article about you and your practice, it will give you credibility and will present you as a recognized industry leader. People trust what they see in print, so always make sure anytime you are mentioned, it's in a positive light. To solicit interest in your practice, contact the editor of a local magazine or newspaper.

About fifteen years ago, I was working with one of my clients who was in a high-tech industry. The industry's leading trade publication price for a full-page ad was $10,000, which the client thought was a great deal. I recommended a public relations approach. The client agreed, and I reached out to the publication's editor and proposed my client's story and how they fulfilled a critical need in the marketplace. The Editor found my proposal of value and assigned his favorite freelancer to write the article. My client was happy with the ten-page article with photos about his business in this exclusive publication. The total cost to my client was the lunch I purchased for the writer when they visited the client's business location. Quite a bargain for a maximum amount of exposure in my client's key industry trade publication.

If you feel you have a story to tell, begin by identifying the publications that serve your area. You can find the local magazines and newspapers at the library, the Chambers of Commerce, as well as magazines and newspapers and periodicals. Don't overlook the free publications; they offer you a wealth of exposure. You will be able to find the publication's editor's name and contact information on the table of contents.

Once you have identified a publication, read and study it. Review their media kit to make sure the publication's demographics match your own. Once you find a publication that you feel would be right for you, prepare a pitch to solicit their interest. A pitch is a little longer than your elevator speech. The following are examples of a pitch.

"Today, more and more people are interested in alternative and holistic practices as a way to improve their health. As a yoga instructor (acupuncturist, or holistic practitioner), I can offer your readers insights on a healthy approach to their physical and mental well-being through yoga. If you feel the health benefits of yoga would interest your readership, I'd love to share my information with one of your reporters."

If you are a Medium, may I suggest you begin your pitch with something like: "With the popularity of reality shows like *The Ghost Whisperer* and *The Hollywood Medium,* people are extremely interested in reaching out to loved ones who have passed on. I am a local Medium who can help them connect to loved ones on the other side. I am available to share my knowledge and expertise with one of your reporters."

If you gain the Editor's interest, they will ask questions to ensure your story would be of interest to their readers. If the Editor decides to do a story about you, great! They will send out a reporter or writer and photographer to tell your story.

If the Editor declines interest in doing a story about you, don't take it personally. He or she feels their readership would not be interested in your subject at this time, or they are simply bumping your story for another story of regional interest. Editors have only so much space to work with, and newspapers and magazines are planned months in advance.

If the Editor is not interested in doing a story about you, be sure you advise the Editor that you are willing to be a resource and a local expert for future editorial needs. Send the editor or publisher a thank-you note and your Tip Sheet. A Tip Sheet is a single page of easy-to-read, often bulleted information about you. The Tip Sheet will be covered shortly in a later chapter.

You can, of course, write your own article or hire a freelance journalist to write an editorial piece about you and send it to the publications.

If you make a connection, stay in touch with local Editors and Publishers. Send holiday cards or a note on an article you enjoyed. It's okay to include your latest brochure, newsletter, or announcement or suggest a fresh article about you.

Keep your media contacts in your CRM. A Customer Relationship Manager; more about CRMs in an upcoming chapter. Please note, if it's been a while since you have contacted an Editor, always do a quick check to make sure the Editor is still at the publication. There is nothing worse than contacting a new editor with their predecessor's name on the cover letter. If you discover your previous contact has moved on, introduce yourself to the new editor and find out where the old editor is now employed, as it might be another publication in your area.

Articles, whether they appear in e-publications or print, are great ways to tell your community about you.

If you are featured in an article, save it, frame it, and reprint it for promotional purposes. Post your article in a prominent location in your office, include copies of it in your media kit, have copies available at any speaking engagements or appearances, and send the article in your newsletter. Be sure to publicize your article on all your social media platforms, including your website.

An article featuring you and your business is a great way to garner exposure for you and your practice.

CHAPTER 17

COLLATERAL MATERIAL

As you think about items you will need for your marketing strategy, I'd like to suggest the following mix of printed material, which is referred to as Collateral Material.

Collateral Material covers a wide variety of print materials, to include but not limited to business and networking cards, brochures, flyers, rack cards, newsletters, postcards, door hangers, bookmarks, labels, and stationery packages.

You don't have to create each collateral piece suggested, but do give thought to the ones you feel would best serve you and your practice. Before you put in your print order, contemplate as to how you intend to use each piece, as well as the costs associated with each item.

Business Cards

Business cards are the quintessential business tool, and even in the digital age, as they are your introduction to prospective clients. If you have an online business, I still urge you to have a Business Card or a Networking Card.

The typical Business Card is three and a half inches by two inches. Business cards can be folded, embossed, and printed on card stock. Designs range from simple black text on a standard white business stock to dazzling four-color designs.

Choose a font that is clean and readable.

Your business card should have your contact information, your name, your business name, your contact telephone and fax number, as well as your physical business address if you have one, as well as your email and website.

If you operate online exclusively or just want to share more information about your services, a networking card would work in place of the standard business card.

A Networking Card is the same size as a business card, but instead of showing a physical address, it will show your name, business name, a list of your services, web address, email, and phone number. A Networking Card allows you to share your contact information when meeting new clients or when exchanging your contact information in a professional environment.

When meeting new clients, at business socials, and at speaking engagements, Business Cards are a handy essential when introducing yourself. I recommend VistaPrint.com as another source for designs, promotional items, and printing needs. I have been using them for years and count on them to deliver consistent quality products. Staples, Office Depot, and your local print store are also a resource for your business cards and print needs and will be able to assist you with graphic services as well.

Despite their small size, professional business cards translate into big business for you. And, don't forget to include an electronic version of your business card in the signature line of your email. I'd also recommend you have a logo.

Logo

A logo is a graphic image that represents you and your business practice. There is no mistaking the power of a strong logo and its impact on your brand. You will look more professional with a logo, and your logo be a key player in all your marketing and branding efforts.

Famous logos include but are not limited to the royal Dutch shell of *Shell Oil* Company, the apple of enlightenment and knowing of *Apple*, or the blue bird of *Twitter*. All these logos exemplify and accentuate their brands.

Your logo should be size adaptable. Envision how your logo would appear on a small business card or on a large format.

While it is easy and inexpensive to simply use clip art images, they look like clip art. For a few dollars more, you can get a beautifully designed logo from FiverR.com or your local print shop.

FiveR.com is an online resource where you can find graphic artists and freelancers who offer a wide variety of design services for small to midsize businesses. I have been using them for years. The talented artists at FiverR.com have developed my logos, banners, and several of my book covers, including the cover on this book. I find their artists talented and their services affordable. I know any number of businesses that are very satisfied with their services. I recommend this company for design services.

Also check with VistaPrint.com as another source for designs, logos, promotional items, and printing needs. I have been using and recommending *VistaPrint.com* for decades. You can count on them to deliver consistent, quality products.

QR Codes

A few short years ago, QR codes were all the rage and very popular to print on business cards. QR codes are those cute little hieroglyphic-looking squares located on business cards, cereal boxes, and in magazine advertisements.

A QR code is an abbreviation for Quick Response Code. Place your phone's camera over a QR code, and your mobile phone will scan the code and translate the coded image into information about the business.

One of my favorite examples of a QR code is found on vegetable packaging. When I open the QR code on vegetable packaging, I am provided information about the vegetable, including how to prepare it and hundreds of recipes, which the advertiser hopes will motivate me into buying more of their product.

If you download a QR code next to a painting or sculpture at a museum, the QR Code will immediately provide you more information about the painting or sculpture and the artist.

A QR code at a bus stop provides scheduling information. A restaurant's QR code can give you menu items, pricing, and nutritional information.

In my opinion, QR Codes can have good application when used properly, however for the small new age practice, QR Codes take up a lot of real estate on a small business card. I recommend just posting your web address on your business cards.

Bookmarkers

Bookmarks are a popular and relatively inexpensive promotional item to use as giveaways or handouts. Everyone uses bookmarkers to save their favorite recipe or hold their place in a novel.

Relatively inexpensive bookmarkers are made of card stock and are generally two and a half inches wide by seven and one-eighth inches high. The graphic design of your bookmarker can be as simple or elaborate as you wish.

Make your Bookmarker appealing, and choose graphic designs that best exemplifies your practice. Ask a question on the front of your bookmarker, or showcase your logo and your practice name. On the back, list your contact information including your website, phone number, and address.

I recommend using four colors on the front to enhance your graphics and black-and-white on the back. It will save costs.

Think of your Bookmarker as a mini-billboard, one the recipient will keep over the life of their book or longer. Like a billboard, keep your message to five to seven words and make your message interesting and intriguing.

For example, if you are a Medium, offer a simple phrase like "Messages from Heaven" on the front of your bookmarker and business location or website on the back.

If you are an Angel Card Reader or Life Coach, "Angels are near when Feathers Appear" or "Every day is a New Beginning" on the front, with your practice name and website and contact information on the back.

Your Bookmarker can be used to promote events and speaking engagements and can be made available at libraries or anywhere books are sold. Always make sure you have the permission of the Bookstore Owner or Librarian before you leave your Bookmarks at their locations.

Brochure

A Brochure is an informative document that provides readers with more information about you and your services. Generally printed on slick or glossy paper, most brochures are 8.5 x 11, which can fold to 8.5 x 5.5 or 8.5 x 3.68.

Some brochures are folded once, while others have a gatefold. Brochures that are gate folded are commonly 11 x 17, then folded to 8.5, folded to 3.68. Brochures are folded to fit nicely into a number ten business envelope. Glossy paper will make your photos stand out. You will generally find brochures at hotels, Chambers of Commences and at other locations where business literature is offered.

When we think of brochures, a hotel brochure is a classic example. A hotel brochure takes advantage of color photographs to showcase the hotel, the rooms, dining, and amenities.

Glossy paper will make your brochure's photos standout.

If you don't have Print Shop or another type of design software, you can have a brochure designed by a freelance graphic designer at FiverR.com or any local printer. There are any number of Brochure templates available online if you'd like to create your own.

Brochures are generally ordered in large quantities, but you can obtain a limited quantity of brochures at VistaPrint.com.

A four-color brochure is a luxury promotional item for small business practices and can be a bit pricy. Most small business use their websites as their brochure. I do not have a brochure; like most small practices, I use my website and blogs as my brochure.

Brochures can be a more expensive piece for the small business, but if you feel like it would benefit your business, consider them.

Flyers

A Flyer can be a simple one-page promotional piece that can be sent by mail or as a standalone promotional piece. Most flyers are black and white; some have a splash of color. While you can print them from your own printer, I recommend taking advantage of a local print and copy shop, especially on days they offer a discounted price for copies.

A Flyer can be as simple as an eight-and-a-half-by-eleven standalone piece or can be eleven by seventeen folded. Flyers can be printed in either color or black and white. If you use black ink for your text, consider a ream of colored paper to make your Flyer stand out.

Flyers can be used to promote special events, for instance a Psychic Fair, posted in a window, used as a mailer, or used as a handout. If you use them at an event, have them padded by your local printer. Padding will keep them at your table and not flying about.

Flyers are a cost-effective alternative to Brochures, and you can print them in quantities as needed.

Postcards

I love Postcards as a standalone or direct mail piece. I created a postcard for each one of my books. The front features my book cover, and the back showcases information about the novel and ordering information. The front cover is in color, and the back is printed in black and white. I hand them out at book signings and events, place them inside of books, as well as using them as mailers.

Postcards work great as handouts. I order my postcards from *VistaPrint.com*, but you can order them anywhere.

If you plan to mail Postcards, they must meet US Postcard standards and are less expensive than cards or letters. As of this date, it costs fifty-five cents to mail a first-class letter versus a postcard which is thirty-five cents.

The standard postcard size is three and a half by five inches or four and a quarter by six inches. Any size larger is in the letter category and will cost more to mail.

Postcards are relatively inexpensive and are perfect for announcing store openings, events, promotions, or special sale dates.

Postcards can be used in lieu of bookmarkers and are a great way to promote your spiritual practice.

Rack Card

Like a brochure, a Rack Card is a printed advertising piece that is typically sized four inches by nine inches.

Rack Cards are usually printed on a heavier card stock and are perfect for mailing or slipped into a point-of-purchase display. Point-of-Purchase displays are usually found at the checkout register or other high-traffic locations within a store, where purchases or add-on decisions are made by a consumer.

Rack Cards are a great way to promote and cross-promote your services at events or as standalones in plastic displays around your store.

Brochures, Rack Cards, and any direct mail piece can be used to promote your speaking engagement, upcoming releases to your customers, or offered at events.

Indoor Signs

Signs have been storefront fixtures since Roman Legions marched across Europe. First-century merchants used eye-grabbing graphics to lure in weary travelers for ale, mutton, and a place to rest.

Today signage does not stop at the door. In-store signage includes tent cards and pop-up display cards placed about your location and is a great way to promote clearance items, special offerings, or advertisements for upcoming events.

Tent Cards are small, triangular table displays. They are folded like small tents, placed on tables or countertops, and printed on both sides of the tent. Restaurants use table tent cards for special offerings of desserts or the wine menu.

This following section is devoted to indoor signs and for signage you display on your personal vehicles. I will have more information for you on Outdoor Signage in a later chapter.

Automobile and Vehicle Signage

Automobile magnetic signage is popular and available from local print shops or online stores such as Vista Print.com.

If you decide to purchase a magnetic sign for your vehicle, make sure the colors stand out and do not blend into obscurity with your car's color.

Keep the message on your automobile's sign short and simple. Too much verbiage makes your sign cluttered, unreadable, and ineffective. One of my pet peeves is to see a car's magnet sign with so much information it renders the message useless. Less is more on your magnetic auto sign.

Car magnets are removable when you want to be off duty or can work twenty-four hours a day for you and your business. If you want to get noticed, consider a full-size window decal for your car's back or side window. Make sure it's legal to cover your back window in your state; while your back-window display is visible to other drivers, you should be able to see through it to watch traffic behind you.

Full automobile wraps are very expensive, permanent, and not removable. With exposure to the sun and elements, they will fade, and you will have to have them replaced, which I mention again, is costly.

Clear Plastic Automobile Business Card Holder

I'd like to strongly suggest you purchase a clear plastic or acrylic rainproof outdoor business card holder for your car. Make your outdoor holders stand out with a "Take One" decal placed just above your card holder.

Plastic card holders attach to the outside of your car. These plastic or acrylic business card holders invite consumers to "Take One" of your business or networking cards. You will be delighted to find how many people take advantage of your card from your weatherproof holder!

Whether you are at the mall, the grocery store, or at a trade show or event, potential customers will grab a business card from this convenient cardholder. Larger acrylic or plastic card holders are also available for brochures, rack cards, or postcards.

I think these larger plastic holders are a great little promotional offering outside your door when your store is closed. I predict you will be amazed how many times you will have to refill your plastic holder when you undertake this promotional opportunity to advertise your practice.

Last but certainly not least, I'd like to recommend Bumper stickers.

Bumper Stickers

Bumper stickers are an inexpensive, easy way to promote your business with an engaging catch phrase like "I stop for Unicorns" or "I stop for Fairies," "Find Joy," or health, or just a lovely graphic with the name of your spiritual practice and website on the bumper sticker. If you teach yoga, a yoga pose would be perfect.

Bumper Stickers are relatively inexpensive, so you can give them to your clients, your family, and your friends. Bumper Stickers are mini-rolling billboards for your practice and provides you with personal endorsements by the car's driver.

As you design your Bumper Sticker, remember to keep your message simple. Use an eye-catching phrase with simple, easy-to-read graphics.

Signs—Banners, Retractable Signs, and Trade Show Signage

Retractable signs are lightweight portable banner signs that pop up or roll out from a retractable base or stand. Retractable signs come with their own carrying case and can be assemble in seconds. They provide you with a dramatic backdrop at speaking engagements or any event you attend.

Retractable signs can stretch from the floor to a full eighty-inch height with a thirty-three-inch width. A smaller version of a Retractable tabletop signs make nice-looking backdrops for online readings or in your store. Both sizes are easy to use and carry with you and are adaptable for use at your store.

If you are engaged with customers at an event, your banner will allow passersby to learn about you and your practice.

Retractable signs are easy to transport and provide you with a smart-looking backdrop at booths or dramatic displays at speaking engagements and are ideal in shops or at events.

Other event signage includes but is not limited to foam signs, posters, tablecloths, and banners.

One of my favorites is a full-length fitted tablecloth. A fitted tablecloth fits snugly over the length of the table and sets you apart from others present. Amazon carries a wide variety of solid colors, but I recommend you personalize your fitted tablecloth with your logo and practice name. You can purchase customized tablecloths from VistaPrint or at local printers that service the trade show industry. Fitted tablecloths will give you a professional look and are a great place to hide boxes you bring to your event.

Small or large signs make your booth or speaking events more dramatic, polished, and professional.

Signs are everywhere; be sure you have the sign exposure to get yourself noticed.

CHAPTER 18

CONTESTS—REAL WORLD AND ONLINE

Contests are a great way to drive traffic to your website and publicize your practice. Offering a contest or participating in an auction, providing a door prize at local meetings will help you bring attention to your practice and clients through your door. Contests help support your brand, reinforces name recognition, and helps you get you noticed.

Whether in the Real World or Online, require all contest participants to register with their email as part of your contest rules. This will allow you to contact participants for contests, newsletters, and special announcements.

Real-World Contests

Contests, auctions, and prizes are a cost-effective marketing strategy to garner attention to your practice. This category includes offering gift baskets to local groups, charitable organizations, conferences, and events.

You can find groups and conferences through an internet search, reaching out to Chamber of Commences, look for charitable groups that have fundraisers to support their cause.

Once you have identified a group, reach out to the group and coordinate and plan out your door prize for the organization.

Theme your goody basket around your practice. Items could include crystals, angel figurines, teas, a cup and saucer, or candles instead of a free reading. I am not a fan of constantly giving away free readings, as it diminishes the value of your services.

As the group or organization promotes the fundraiser, members will hear about your offering and your practice. Extend the value of your basket by offering those who did not win a special, limited-time discount. This extends the reach of your giveaway to the membership of an organization and consequently prompts interest and appointments for your practice.

Once at a state fishing organization's annual fundraiser, I donated a basket filled with my popular romance novels. My donation earned me a wealth of free publicity and bolstered book sales. It was personally gratifying to know the donations for my basket contributed to help support clean rivers in my state.

Keep a record of what type of groups offer such events, and keep track of the response. If you get a good response from your gift, do it again. If you do not get a good response, consider other opportunities to get your name noticed.

If you are at a speaking engagement and want to give a free reading as a door prize, I'm okay with that, as it will create excitement and prompt others in attendance to schedule an appointment with you. In this scenario, offer a group discount rate good for the day of the event or a few days after. I'll have additional tips for public speaking later in this section.

Radio and PBS stations are always on the lookout for free gifts. Contact the prize coordinator and offer a free reading or gift basket for on-air promotion. You might be invited to the station for an on-air interview. Steer clear of shock jocks who will try to have fun at your expense.

Contests can include fundraisers where you are not present, for instance offering a basket or gift at your local PBS station.

If you plan on participating in New Age Events or festivals, find out if there is an opportunity to reach attendees though an auction or giveaway. If you participate a festival or event, have a fishbowl at your table or booth. Have everyone who registers for your item provide their name, phone number, and email address. Never offer a prize at an event or on your website without capturing their names and emails.

I also like to suggest in addition to the contestant's name and email address, ask for their day and month of birth; do not ask for the year. By asking for this information, you can reach out to those same contestants for special offers, birthday greetings, as well as holiday cards and special promotions you are having. I'll have more about information on contests in this venue in the chapter on Event Marketing.

Like good advertising, good contests are only good if they bring in customers through your door. Contests are a great way to get noticed and draw attention to your practice. The cost of a goody basket or prize giveaway should be well under twenty dollars; however, the exposure it brings is priceless, as well as the wealth of good public relations you will draw to for this relatively small investment.

Online Contests

To drive traffic and customers to your website, offer an online contest. As previously mentioned, as part of your contest rules, have your contestants register for your contest with their email. By having your contestants register, they are giving you permission to contact them about your current contest and others you will have in the future. This allows you to send out messages, offer discounts, special promotions, and your newsletters. The marketing term for this is called permission marketing.

If you are just getting started and want the practice, you can offer free readings; just be sure you capture emails of those who register for your contest. Once you are established, I frown on constantly offering free readings, as it diminishes the value of your services. Free readings attract people who will troll your site for free readings and contest junkies who will never pay you for your services; they simply bide their time until another free-reading contest comes along. Free readings should be reserved for when you are practicing your skills only.

I would recommend you to offer small gifts such as a book, crystals, figurines, oils, or a gift that has a connection with and supports with your practice.

The goal of your contest is to drive people to your website and promote your practice. Contests are a great way to generate new business, spread the word about your practice, and promote your services. Promote your contests on your website and on all your social media platforms, including Pinterest, Twitter, Facebook, and Instagram.

Converting Contest Players into Paying Customers

You can only have one contest winner, but through your contest registration, you gathered hundreds of names and email addresses. Reach out with an inviting discount to every registered contest participant who didn't win. For example, send out an email with reads, "Judy Z of Australia won my monthly contest, but I would like to offer you a special discount!" and present your offer. Set a time limit on your offer; this creates urgency and a call to action. Send this offer just to the people who registered for your contest, not everyone on client list. Your email should include a link to schedule an appointment and a link to your PayPal or payment link.

In the sales arena, there are two practices I want you to become familiar with. One is upselling, which happens every time a sales associate asks if you'd like fries with that burger. The other technique is asking for the sale. As an entrepreneur, you need to learn both.

An example of an upsell is, "If you take advantage of this special offer, I'll give you a second reading at a 50 percent discount" or "Buy One, Give One" or "Buy One, Get a Second One Free." Do not leave your offer open indefinitely; create urgency with, as mentioned, a call to action. A call to action is, if today is July 1, "This offer is good only till July 3."

If your business is a retail store, you and your sales staff should be upselling on every purchase. For example, as a patron is checking out, say, "I love this crystal you are purchasing, did you notice the crystal pendulums are on sale today?" Always add on another item to the purchase.

As a Psychic or Spiritual Practitioner, you will always be tapped by a group of people who want to solicit your advice for free outside your practice hours. I get that it's in your nature to help, and it's always a kind gesture if you choose to do so; however, if someone is constantly seeking advice, convert them to a paying customer with the following statement.

In the Real World, when someone asks for a reading, say: "I'm not in front of my appointment book at the moment, so could you call me later to schedule an appointment?" or "This is a great question, one that needs a bit more time than I have now. Let's go in depth during an appointment."

With an online inquiry, I follow up with "I'd be happy to schedule an appointment with you" and then send them an email to include a scheduling link and a link to your PayPal or payment link.

Converting contest participants is a great way to increase your bottom line. Where do I register for your next contest?

CHAPTER 19

CRM—CUSTOMER RELATIONSHIP MANAGEMENT SYSTEM

This is a short chapter but an important one. A CRM is a customer relationship management system. A CRM software program, one that fulfills an important aspect of customer management, whether real world or on the web.

A CRM is a business necessity that maintains your clients' information in a professional, organized database. Your CRM allows you to record your client's name, address, phone, and email into a database, as well as help you in managing appointments and day-to-day tasks and activities. CRM software will also help you set business goals and predict financial forecasts.

Years ago, as an outside salesperson, I, like many of my counterparts, had to rely on index cards or cumbersome file folders to keep track of customer records and information. They were difficult to track and easy to misplace between the car and the office.

Today, there are any number types of sophisticated software to give you instant and easy access to customer records and create special email or mailing lists directly from your CRM system.

There are many elaborate and sophisticated customer relations software programs to choose from to help you with current customer management, managing tasks, to-do lists, and potential clients. Everyone has their preference, generally based on what they are most familiar in using and cost. Popular CRM software includes ACT, Salesforce, and Goldmine, to name a few. I have been recommending ACT for years. ACT is simple and easy to use, and I like easy and simple.

With your CRM, you can generate emails or print out mailing labels to your entire customer base or create separate promotions to potential clients. You do this by filtering specific fields in your CRM. You can also modify your filter to distinguish your Media list.

Your CRM is the life force of your business, as it will allow you to effectively manage your clients and prospective customers, as well as maintain records, appointments, tasks, and schedules. A good CRM software system is an excellent way to help you organize your practice and assist you in customer retention.

Like business cards, I believe a good CRM system is a business must! Do an online review of CRM or visit your local technology store for recommendations that will work for you.

CHAPTER 20

DIRECT MAIL AND EMAIL BLASTS

If your mailbox is like mine, it's loaded with all sorts of direct mail pieces, which are often referred to as junk mail. A Direct Mail piece can be a flyer, letter, brochure, postcard, or any other printed material that is delivered through the US Postal Service.

You receive Direct Mail because of where you live, zip code locale, and fit a specific demographic group. I live close to a major shopping center, and my mailbox is filled with coupons, flyers, and restaurant discounts from the stores located there.

In my professional life, I have purchased and used Direct Mail many times to promote my clients. I used Direct Mail because it works when it's targeted to the right market. A successful average response on a direct mail campaign can range from 1 percent to 5 percent and as high as 7 percent response. The average response or return on investment is 3 percent. That may sound low, but in a direct mail campaign, as you consider costs versus return, the 3 percent response is considered very good.

My husband is an avid fisherman, and he subscribes to several fishing magazines. Magazines sometimes sell their list of subscribers to companies that sell fishing products, and so my husband happily receives all sorts of offers on lures, fishing tackle, and outdoor gear.

You can purchase a mailing list from any local Direct Mail house or online. As I was researching information for this book, I found several companies online that specialize in the New Age Market. These companies obtain their mailing lists from new age publications and businesses that sell their subscribers lists. I personally don't mind receiving information about new products or services, as I am always interested in hearing about new offerings in a market that interests me.

When using a Direct Mail house, you can purchase everyone in a zip code area or refine your mailing list to everyone in your town who owns a red car. Meet with a representative to discuss what would work best for your practice, and make sure you understand all costs. All costs include development of your direct mail piece; the printing; the cost of the mailing list, which you rent, not buy; and as well as postage and mailing. Compare costs of preparing your own direct mail piece, printing it, and delivering to the Direct Mail house with the cost the Direct Mail house will charge you for developing it at their location.

Just to be clear, the list you purchase is not yours to use to perpetuity. Nor will the list be given to you; the Direct Mail house will always retain possession of your mailing list. If you rent or "buy" your list more than one time, you will likely receive a discount on the price.

Once you have decided on whom you wish to target, contact a direct mail house and tell them who you are and what sort of list you are looking for. Be precise. You may be able to find a list with telephone numbers for a telemarketing follow-up campaign.

You can create your own Direct Mail campaign by pulling from your clients and potential customers from your database. Sending out a postcard, flyer, or incentive to people who are familiar with you will typically generate a higher response.

If you have addresses and emails, don't overload a customer's inbox or mailbox with communications, as it's a quick way to have your messages blocked and your mail or email quickly discarded.

I recommend sending out a mailed piece several times a year to your customers. I touch base with my clients with holiday cards, birthday cards, newsletters, or promotional offers. Sending out these cards and offers will encourage repeat business and keep you top of mind.

Whether you purchase a direct mail list or send your mailers out to customers, your message should include a strong call to action. A call to action is a highlighted or comment bubble that reads "Call Today for an Appointment," "Space is Limited," or "Sale ends July 6!"

Some Direct Mail pieces are created to say thank you, encourage repeat business, and keeps you top of mind to new and potential customers.

Target your customers and target market your direct mail recipients with the right message at the right time. Calculate the costs you incurred to create and mail them, and anticipate your response.

Email Marketing

While on the topic of Direct Mail, I'd like to discuss Email Marketing. Email, of course, refers to electronic mail sent from your web address. You stay in touch with your customers and potential clients through email.

As previously stated, obtain permission to send out emails. You can obtain your customers' emails by collecting email as contestants register for your contests, sign up for your newsletters, and gave you their emails from any events you attend.

E-Mail Blasts can include but are not exclusive to sending out promotional announcements of chats, new products, newsletters, and contests. You can manage your email, direct mail, and contact list though a CRM system.

Direct Mail and Emails are important tools in your marketing arsenal. They are easy to use, inexpensive, helps you stay in touch with your customers, and stimulates sales.

Keep your Direct Mail and Email list up to date by asking customers if their email or address has changed if a piece returns to you. Include mailing dates and times of year in your promotional calendar, so you won't miss an opportunity to connect to your customers.

CHAPTER 21

EVENT MARKETING

Event Marketing is one of the most attention-grabbing, high-profile strategies to promote your practice. Whether you participate in an event, festival, or public-speaking opportunity, Event Marketing offers you an extraordinary opportunity to be the star of the show.

Begin by identifying any local or regional event marketing opportunities, and note the dates in your promotional calendar. New Age Events and Psychic Fairs are natural venues for you to connect to a target-rich environment, as those in attendance are already predisposed to the New Age products and services.

As a Fairyologist and Environmental Educator, I look forward to participating in Earth Day Celebrations. At these events, I share information on the importance of recycling, protecting animals, and the environment.

You may already be aware of Psychic Fairs in your area, but you can identify other venues by contacting your local Chamber of Commerce, your area's convention centers, or simply do an internet search for New Age Festivals.

If you participate in a Fair or Event, be sure to bring plenty of collateral materials for guests who will stop by your booth or register for a giveaway. Bring your appointment calendar to schedule appointments. Don't forget to make your booth sparkle with signage!

There are also many additional regional events and festivals that can work for you. For instance, at a Renaissance Fair, you can market your crystals and card readings to attendees. If you do attend such a festival, have fun and wear appropriate attire suited for the event.

Bridal Fairs are a target-rich environment to offer readings or schedule consultations. Bridal Fairs are also a good fit to sell jewelry as well as any spiritual practices that offer weight loss, health, and wellness.

Street carnivals, Art and Book Fairs will also present fresh opportunities to meet and attract new customers.

When considering an event, ask the Event Coordinator about the attendance of previous years and how many participants are expected at any new event. This will not only help you in understanding the amount of collateral materials to bring but provide you with the insight you need to help in forecasting how much new business you can expect from a successful turnout.

Ask the event organizer's marketing and promotional plans. Look for opportunities in which you can participate in such as any pre-event publicity such as television experience or public-speaking opportunity at the event, and of course the availability of being featured in a prominent ad in the program.

As you consider this opportunity, find out whether tables or booths are provided and if tablecloths are included. If tablecloths are not available, be sure to bring your own tablecloth with your name and logo across the front.

Not all events offer booths or tables, so understand exactly what each venue provides. If it's an outdoor event, you may want to bring a canopy to offer shelter from the elements.

Gather all costs associated with the event, to make sure they work for you.

If indoors, consider adding extra padding in your area. Most arenas and outdoor venues have hard cement flooring, so extra padding will make your area more comfortable for tired feet. Studies show visitors will stay longer at your booth if you make it comfortable for them.

To offset the costs of a festival or event, consider sharing your booth with a friend or business associate. The ideal colleague would be someone who compliments your practice, but not a direct competitor unless you both agree to how to handle customers who visit your booth.

Register early! Those who register early will have their choice of prime locations. If you wait until the last moment to register, you may find yourself in an obscure corner or far away from the main traffic flow.

If you are attending a large event, bring extra help to assist you. Review the chapter on signage.

I recommend offering water or soft drinks for sale at your location. This add-on won't bring in huge profits, but it will give attendees a reason to stop and learn more about your practice. Attach a label with your practice name on the bottles. Others who notice the bottles will also take note of your practice, but the primary benefit is attracting visitors to your location.

Contact the local media ahead of the event, to encourage them to do a story about you, and let them know your booth number and location.

Send Press Releases to the Editors of all media in the area. I'd often get the lion's share of publicity as I dropped off a press kit and press release along with a basket of pastries to the local newspaper. If you decide to take a goody basket to a station, don't leave it at the front desk; make sure you hand it to an editor or television producer.

Drop off a flyers, postcards, or event brochure at any New Age bookstores or health-food stores you frequent. Make sure you highlight your practice name and booth number.

Invite participants to register for a nice prize at your booth, and ask registrants for their name, email address, and or phone number. Have your local printer print up your coupons and pad them so they won't fly about.

I am not a big fan of cheap items such as pens, keychains, and bottle openers. Inexpensive promotional items are aimlessly gathered by attendees and forgotten as soon as they reach home. Inexpensive items yield very little return on their investment.

When offering a free prize, consider a piece of nice jewelry or goody basket or even a free reading.

If you plan to have music, play it loud enough to attract attention but not so loud that you have to shout over your music to speak to attendees.

You will find more information to help you in planning an event in the Promotional Calendar Chapter in Part IV of this book. However, let me touch on the importance of preplanning for the event. Preplanning gives you sufficient time to prepare the collateral materials, signage you will need, as well as creating flyers and postcards promoting your event. Preplanning will make each event a success.

The day of the event, make sure your area is inviting. Take photos of you at the event, especially if a small crowd is visiting. These photos will come in handy for future marketing initiatives. If you do take pictures, have a small sign stating you will be taking photos. If you post a photo on your website, make sure you have permission.

Whether you are participating in an outdoor venue, New Age Fair, Flea Market, or even at your store location, provide your clients with a way to pay for your services or products with their debit or credit cards. PayPal or Square are two of the most popular payment systems. Find a payment plan that works for you. These companies and others like them charge a relatively small transaction fee, but increased sales will far outweigh any small transaction charge, so if you are attending an event, be prepared to accept payments.

Once at a Meet-the-Authors Event at a popular local park, more than forty authors were in attendance, but only a fraction of those authors had brought their own bank for attendees to purchase books. Many authors who brought a bank continuously ran out of small denominations throughout the day and lost sales because of it. I had prepared with both a money bag and a Square to capture credit cards and was happily prepared to accept payments. I actually sold quite a number of books. Plan the work, work the plan!

At the event, know the venue. Be able to direct attendees to the bathrooms, food and drink locations, and exits. Have extra programs or event maps at your location, and be sure to attach your flyer or business card to any information you hand out.

After the event, thank the organizers, send out a thank-you note to everyone who stopped by your booth, as well as recording their names in your CRM manager system.

You are almost done! Go back to every online platform where you promoted your event, and post how successful the event was for you. This post follow-up will continue to draw attention to you and your practice.

Last, but certainly not least, evaluate your performance, and make note of any clever marketing ideas you want incorporate into future event-marketing opportunities. Then, be sure to pat yourself on the back for undertaking this marketing strategy.

Small Events—The Psychic Tea Party

You don't always have to attend large events to bring in customers to your practice. Sometimes a small event will bring the attention and new clients your desire. A Psychic Tea or Afternoon Tea might be the perfect marketing strategy, especially if you prefer small informal events.

Whether you do it once a week, once a month, or once every quarter, Psychic Tea Parties or an Afternoon Tea might be just the pick-me-up your practice needs. I recommend you create a theme for each Psychic Tea Party. Themes allow you to focus on topic and make each tea a unique.

Look at your Promotional Calendar and decide what monthly or quarterly themes work for you. I recommend drawing from the holidays found in each month. For instance, a January Tea Party would spark interest in new beginnings and new goals. February is the perfect time to host a Tea Party focused on romance. On or around St. Patrick's Day, discuss Celtic legends or fairies. April brings spring celebrations and a second time to jump-start goals and ambitions. You get the idea. Use each month's dominant holiday to showcase various aspects of your spiritual practice.

Tea Parties can be elegant and grand affairs or comfortable, cozy gatherings. Make each event unique and different from the one before.

Tea Parties should be welcoming. Customers and new clientele feel more at home in a group setting. Encourage your guests to bring a friend, and have a signup sheet to guarantee seating and commitment. Send out email reminders of your scheduled event.

Your Psychic or Wellness Tea Party should have a start and end time; after all, you still have a spiritual practice to run and appointments to keep.

I recommend you begin your Tea with a group meditation or invocation, followed by your presentation. After your presentation, allow time for a question-and-answer session, as well as a time for attendees to socialize, a chance to visit your store and get a taste of you and your services.

If you plan on regularly hosting a Tea Party, consider ordering a couple dozen imprinted mugs or coffee cups for your teas. You can reuse the cups and even offer them for sale at your store or to an online viewing party.

Hosting a Tea Party allows you to create a community of customers who support you and who will recommend you to their friends.

If you don't have a location to host your Tea Party, scout out local tea rooms, small restaurants, or cafés. The managers of these locations might very well welcome an opportunity to reach new customers, especially on those days or afternoons when their business is slow.

An alternate setting could be your home, the home of a friend or neighbor, but before you post the address, know who will be coming. Offer your host or hostess a free reading for hosting the event, or be sure to thank them with a gift or goody basket. Have attendees chip in for refreshments supplied by you or the hostess.

If you host a Psychic Tea Party, light refreshments are in order. I suggest a variety of teas and light refreshments, as well as a couple of small giveaways. Stage your event with simple decorations. Flowers, scented oils, or candles will foster ambiance as well as depth, warmth, and elegance for the meeting.

If you are a Yoga Instructor, you might want to consider specialize miniworkouts for the back and shoulders or to reduce stress.

If you sell herbs or oils, share information about the healing properties of herbs and natural remedies and offer a special price the day of the event to encourage sales.

If you are an Angel, Tarot, or Crystal Card Reader, invite each guest to choose a single card for a one-card reading.

If you own a crystal shop or store, you may want to focus on a crystal of the month and how it is used in healing and manifestation. If you are a psychic, explain the "clairs," or focus on monthly or seasonal themes. If you are Medium, share messages you receive with the attendees.

Have attendees RVSP. Their response is not only a reservation but helps you plan and prepare for those who will attend. You will need to know how many RSVP to ensure sufficient gifts and refreshments and always plan for walk-ins.

Play your favorite music before you start your event, softly during any meditation, and at the conclusion of your meeting.

Invite business friends, not in your industry, to showcase their businesses, and make sure you have a reciprocal agreement with their clients.

Have every attendee register, and make sure you capture their name, email, and note their interests. If you like, offer fun door prizes or a raffle.

Use photos of your Tea Party to promote your spiritual practice on all your social media platforms.

Send out flyers, emails, and promote your event at your location. Mention your Psychic Tea Party at any event you attend.

If you have a Meetup Group, post and promote your event there. Post your Tea on any community calendars and newspapers, and contact those publications for a promotional article about your event.

Whatever your skill or practice, you can build a Tea Party or small workshop around it. Tea Parties are social events for fun and profit!

CHAPTER 22

NEWSLETTERS AND E-NEWSLETTERS

Newsletters and e-newsletters are an excellent way to stay in touch with your clients, prompt repeat business, and showcase your services to your customers. Your newsletters are an extension of your brand, so keep the same look and feel consistent with your brand. Whether you use a template or create your own, your newsletter should be fun, interesting to read, and focused on your practice.

Make your newsletter timely and relevant, and deliver when promised. You can set your own schedule, whether it's monthly, every six weeks, or quarterly.

Newsletters can be short and chatty or lengthy. The style depends on you. Make your font easy to read, print black and white, and if you like, add a splash of color on the front page.

I recommend you choose a theme for each newsletter, and that theme should expand on an aspect of your practice or when introducing a new product or service. Make sure you include your contact information, your website, blog, Twitter, or Facebook accounts in your newsletter.

You can spotlight a guest or business associate with whom you have an affinity alliance.

Your Newsletter is also a great place to promote your upcoming appearances, engagements, and events. Contests and coupons within your newsletter are other promotional opportunities to encourage patronage.

In your newsletter, offer book reviews of authors in your field. If you decide to include a book review, coordinate your review with your local bookseller, who may invite you to leave copies of your newsletters at their location.

Another great idea comes from an author friend who built her readership by sending out recipe cards every month, so, if you like, include a recipe of the month based on your monthly theme.

Ask intriguing questions in your newsletter to engage with your readers and prompt return visits. Post links to your newsletter on all your social media platforms, and in your e-newsletters, add in links to your products and website.

Ask New Age Book Stores, coffee shops, cafés, libraries, and other locations if you can leave copies of your newsletters at their locations.

If your Newsletter is available online, print out a few copies for use at speaking engagements or as handouts at events. If you have an office or storefront, make them available to visitors and clients.

Offer Newsletter sign-up sheet at events, speaking locations, and on your website. Advertisements can offset your newsletter production costs. If you do decide to offer advertisements in your newsletter, keep them to a minimum, as you don't want your information lost in a clutter of ads.

Newsletters are an effective way to build your customer base, keep in touch with your current clients, and reach out to future customers.

CHAPTER 23

OUTDOOR ADVERTISING

I have already covered indoor promotional signage in the chapter on collateral materials, which encompasses signage in stores, at events, and at trade shows. I'd now like to share advertising opportunities in outdoor, transit, and roadside signage.

Outdoor signage includes signs devoted to draw attention and traffic to your practice and can be as simple as a realtor or yard sign or a chalkboard sign promoting your retail location.

Some of the outdoor signage in the following pages will fit your budget, while others may be outside your advertising budget. Let's explore Outdoor Signs that might work for you.

Billboards

Billboards are the advertising giants that stare at us as we drive our cars on city streets and interstate highways. Billboards line our roadways and are seen by drivers, vehicle passengers, and anyone traveling our streets. They are attention-getters, especially if located at busy intersections where consumers wait for the traffic lights to change. Typically, they measure 14 feet high and 48 feet wide, encompassing a full 672 square feet of advertising space.

If you decide to explore this venue, be aware that Billboard messaging relies on strong graphic images. Professionals will advise to keep your advertising copy to five to seven words. Choose colors that will stand out against a light blue or darkening sky.

Like real estate, Billboards and Billboard prices rely on location, location, location and the volume of traffic that passes by each board in a twenty-four-hour period. This figure is generally calculated by city and county transportation authorities.

Other factors include traffic speed, the billboard's proximity to the road, and impressions. Impressions is a term used to describe the number of consumers who view each billboard each day. Also pay attention to travelers' destination, which asks if drivers are driving in the direction of your business or driving home.

Billboards located on isolated county roads are less expensive. Lighted billboards are more expensive than unlighted boards, as lighted billboards get exposure both night and day.

Billboard companies can provide you with additional demographics information such as age, gender, and the average income level of people who pass by a billboard. You will pay more in upscale neighborhoods and metropolitan areas than industrial zones.

Traditional billboards can cost between $250 and $550 a month in rural areas and between $1,500 and $5,000 a month in midsize cities. Digital billboards, with their flashy and dazzling graphics, generally start around $3,000 a month up to $10,000 a month, depending on their location in key metropolitan areas. The cost of a billboard is based on the several key factors.

If it's within your budget, secure a Billboard next to your location. If you can purchase such a billboard near your physical location, your copy should read something like, "Turn here for Amy's New Age Emporium."

To locate the owner of the Billboard, look to the center of the sign, which will showcase the owner.

There are two basic types of Billboards, static or traditional billboards and digital billboards. Static billboards are the traditional billboards that display the same graphics for up to two years. Their digital counterparts are attention grabbers with flamboyant graphics and changeable messages, and they are expensive.

Digital signs are also found at indoor and outdoor sports arenas, inside airports providing flight arrivals and departures, and at the movie theater, which announce movie locations within a theater and start times.

While Billboards are attention-getters, they can be very expensive for the small business owner. Let's look at more affordable outdoor advertising options for the small business.

Junior Poster Boards

I like Junior Poster Boards and would frequently purchase them for my mall and retail store clients, especially around key sales periods such as back-to-school or holiday shopping. They are also great for regional sporting events and real-estate openings.

Junior Poster Boards are smaller than billboards, viewed at street level, sizes around ten feet, seven inches by twenty-two feet, nine inches, and are available in freestanding units or mounted on buildings. They can be purchased for shorter time periods and prices range on average from $225 to around $500 for a four-week period.

Junior Poster Boards are purchased in one-, two-, or four-week increments and can sometimes be rented for a longer period. Ask your Junior Poster representative for prices and locations available in your area.

If you can find a Junior Poster board, especially if it's near your locations, it might be worth the buy for a grand opening, big event at your store, or during peak holiday periods.

Bus or Transit Advertising

If you travel through cities across America and the world, you are aware of buses. They are big, bulky and lumber through our streets, stopping it seems every quarter mile to pick-up passengers. They are another component of outdoor advertising, and they are hard to miss as you drive by them or get stuck behind them. They are rolling billboards with powerful graphics that promote upcoming events, realtors, local attorneys, businesses, and products.

There are a variety of options when contemplating bus or transit advertising, from Bus Benches and Bus Shelters ad placements to interior or exterior signage.

The first question when considering any medium is to make sure the type of ad you spend your money on is reaching your target market. The city bus transit demographic states bus riders are typically in the twenty-five to fifty-four age market. Forty percent are white, thirty percent are African American, thirty percent are Hispanic, and the remainder is composed of other cultures and ethnic backgrounds. The ratio will vary and is dependent on where you live in the country. Medium income will also vary but ranges from $15,000 to $45,000. Note this number will fluctuate depending where you live and the geographical size of your area.

Studies indicate that in metropolitan areas, 71 percent of bus riders are employed, 7 percent are students, and most riders are women with college educations. More than half of bus riders state they own their own vehicles but take the bus for the convenience, to avoid the hassles of city traffic and locating a parking space when they reach their destination. Many vehicle owners drop their cars off at Park and Ride locations before boarding a bus.

Bus Advertising reaches a broad market. You want to always stay within your target market. Let's look at other types of advertising in the medium.

Exterior Bus Signs

Exterior Bus Signs are hard to miss as they travel their routes about town, as they are viewed at eye level from the side or back of a bus. Advertising opportunities include the side of a bus, the back of a bus, and not recommended for a small business are the full bus wrap-around signage.

Exterior bus ads range in price from $400 to over $15,000 a month, dependent on the city size. Prices will vary by your city's demographic group. Bus company advertisers will assist you in design, production, and installation.

Exterior Bus signs are rolling billboards with advantages of reaching a lot of consumers. As always, consider your return on investment, routes, and factor in if they reach your market.

Interior Bus Advertising

Inside the bus, passengers have little to do other than look out the window, listen to podcasts, and view their social media platforms on their cell phones. Bus riders are a captive audience—if they fit your target market.

Interior Bus advertising only reaches bus riders during their commute. If you are considering this medium, consider bus companies' demographic data. Interior Bus signs are relatively inexpensive, and a four-week ad campaign can range from $40 to $100 per ad per the length of contract.

Before investing in Interior Bus advertisements, conduct your own market research by riding a bus on a route that is located near you. Do some people watching, and decide if the passengers hit all the check marks in your demographic group. If you feel they are your target market group, try Interior Bus signage for a limited time period, say six weeks, and gauge your return on investment.

Bus Bench and Bus Shelter Advertising Opportunities

Bus benches or shelters may fit into your advertising budget, especially if they are close to your location, visible at busy intersections, or along streets with slow-moving traffic.

This medium offers you street signage that is both highly noticeable and can be very effective in promoting your practice. Rates and terms will vary. If you feel this might be a good investment, contact your local bus company. Sometimes the same companies that manage local billboards will also handle this type of advertising.

Prices for Bus Bench or Shelter advertising can vary, and some companies will offer you a one-week to four-week advertising run. Prices will depend on your city's population and can range $50 to $75 for a four-week purchase. The price will depend on location, duration or length of purchase, and the amount of traffic that passes by the bench's location daily. There may be a minimum purchase required, but if you are interested and can find a bench or shelter close to your practice, this might be an excellent opportunity for you.

Talk to your local bus advertising representative about benches available in your area, the length of time you must commit to, and if they will assist you in design or recommend a graphic designer.

Before you sign any outdoor sign contract, get in your vehicle and conduct your own research of each location. Make sure your bench has good exposure and is visible to drivers and pedestrians. Both should be a target market fit.

If you are satisfied that your bench has good exposure and tap into your demographics, contact the advertising representative for all costs associated with this advertising purchase.

In a world where less is more, Bench or Bus Shelter advertisement might give you the outdoor exposure you are looking for.

Flags Signage

Flag Signage is great, especially for special events, sales, or promotions, or to simply draw attention to your retail location. Flag signs are lightweight, durable outdoor signs that are generally made of polyester and attached to lightweight fiberglass or aluminum poles. They typically come with preprinted messages like "sale," "open," or "welcome."

Flag signs come in a variety of styles such as feathers, teardrops, razors, and traditional rectangular flag shapes. Most notably, feather and razor-style signs are popular with car dealerships when promoting a sale. Outdoor signs are a dramatic way to draw attention to your business.

Realtor and Yard Signs

Realtor Signs were once called Burma Shave signs, as they stood as little advertising markers for Burma Shave that crisscrossed county roads and highways promoting their product.

Today these little signs are used by Realtors and politicians, serve as yard sale signs, and stand in front of businesses to announce a sale. They are portable, durable, and made for outdoor use.

These little signs are small, so keep your message short by showcasing your name, phone number, website, or perhaps a short message such as "Tarot Card Readings $10.00 Today Only." If you work at home but want to promote your practice to the neighborhood, a Realtor-type sign might be just the signage you need; be sure, of course, you have all the necessary requirements for running a home-based business in your area.

These small outdoor signs can promote your spiritual practice or you can use them as to direct drivers to your meeting or location. If you put them out on roadways, remember to bring them in at night, as county inspectors will permanently remove them.

As with a car magnetic sign, keep your message short, make sure your background colors pop and don't blend into a blue sky or a green yard.

Realtor signs are sturdy are quintessential yard or roadside sign and are relatively inexpensive.

Thinking small might reap big results for your bottom line.

Lamp Post Signage

Lamp Post banners are found along city streets and scenic parks around towns. Lamp Post signage is generally reserved for local festivals, holidays, events, as well as late-night pubs.

Lamp Post and street banners hang on lampposts and are most noticeable at night when streetlights showcase this outdoor advertising banner. It is my belief they do not offer you a high return on the financial investment.

However, if you create your own banner to use at your storefront, they serve as an outstanding bit of signage, especially if you use a solar spotlight to shine on it during early evening hours.

Adopt a Street or Highway

While billboards are expensive for the small business, there is a smaller but effective outdoor sign that could work in your behalf and that is an Adopt-a-Street sign, especially if they are close to your brick-and-mortar location.

Adopting a Street is good for the environment and is good public relations for you. This program also saves taxpayers money and supports antilitter education.

Adopt-a-Street signage supports your brand, providing you with outdoor exposure and visibility in your area. In addition to reaching thousands who will view your sign, the Earth Fairies, elementals, and the Universe will appreciate your efforts.

If this initiative sounds appealing, contact your local county or city government. Some local governments charge a small fee, and others do not, as they trade your litter pickups for community cost savings. Check with your local municipalities for any costs or fees in this program.

Most do charge a small fee, and you are expected to commit to litter pickups at least four times a year. The local or county governments take care of permits, providing the Adopt-a-Street Sign as well as all cost associated with your Adopt-a-Street Sign.

Local authorities will also provide you with biodegradable bags, which, after you collect litter, you'll leave beside the roadway for county or city pickup. You may also be required to attend safety meetings. Sponsorship rules vary by municipality.

A quick note, while my husband and I support and participate in Adopt-a-River, Stream, and Hiking Trails, we do so as both a pleasure and privilege, but when promoting the spiritual practice, I recommend sticking to the streets and roads close to your physical location. The city or county governments will help you select a street near you.

Your Adopt-a-Street signage will not only show the community you care, it will support your brand and provides you with good publicity as every time you have a cleanup event which you can publicize across all your social media platforms.

Your sponsorship will be viewed by thousands of locals who pass by your signage and appreciated by customers, Earth guardians, and your community.

CHAPTER 24

THE PRESS KIT

A Press Kit is a packet of information about you and your spiritual practice. You may hear the Press Kit referred to as a Media Kit. There is a very slight difference between the terminology. A Media Kit is a general packet of information prepared for the media, while a Press Kit offers specifically targeted information for an event. Today, most people simply use the term Press Kit as I do now.

Press Kits are typically created for members of the media, including reporters or editors of the press, which includes newspapers, magazines, radio, and television. Its purpose is to inform the media and generate interest about you. Press Kits are also useful when presenting yourself to a group facilitator at a speaking engagement or event coordinator.

Whether you build your own Press Kit or hire a publicist, an advertising or public relations firm to help you, you will look more professional.

To create your own Press Kit, I'd first recommend you purchase a quality folder from your office-supply store. VistaPrint.com and other online companies offer customized folders.

If you built your own kit, I'd like to suggest you order and affix your own crack-and-peel label for the front cover.

Crack-and-peel labels are like address labels. In the early days of advertising, you'd have to crack labels away from paper, hence the name crack and peel. Crack-and-peel labels come in rolls or flat sheets. Combined with a nice-looking folder, a crack-and-peel image of your logo is an affordable alternative to preprinted pocket folders. I recommend clear Crack-and peel labels with your name and logo prominently placed in the center.

The following items should be included in your Press Kit.

1. A current Press Release
2. Past or Current Articles about you
3. A short Biography
4. Photographs of you (Black-and-White or Color)
5. Contact Information, to include your website
6. List of any upcoming events or personal appearances
7. A FAQ Sheet
8. Any Collateral Materials— Brochures, Flyers, Postcards, etc.
9. Your most recent Newsletter
10. A Tip Sheet

A Tip Sheet is a one-page marketing essential, and if you choose to forgo the Press Kit, your Tip Sheet will work nicely in its place.

Offer an online version on your website, and always have several Press Kit on hand as you will never know when a newspaper or broadcast representative may reach out to you with an offer to showcase your practice.

Tip Sheet

Tip Sheet is a one-page document that offers a quick overview of your practice and services.

Information on your Tip Sheet is generally designed in a bulleted format. As a marketing tool, a Tip Sheet will showcase your business profile to media, used as a companion piece with your press release or left with an event organizer.

Your Tip Sheet should include but is not limited to the following information:

1) Your Practice Name
2) Your Head Shot, Logo, or both
3) Contact Information

4) A short Biography of you
5) Your Company's Profile or List of Services
6) A complete list of your Social Media sites, to include your Facebook, Twitter, Instagram, Blog, and Website

A Tip Sheet is a great leave-behind when introducing yourself to a group or event coordinator or as a standalone marketing tool to anyone who wants to learn more about you.

CHAPTER 25

PRESS RELEASES

A Press Release is a news story or special announcement sent to newspapers and media outlets. Press releases are a cost-effective marketing strategy that offers you a wealth of free publicity and an exposure.

Press Releases can be mailed, emailed, or faxed.

Your Press Release should be interesting and newsworthy. Newsworthy events include but are not limited to a store opening, new products, special events, anniversaries, new hires, awards, and personal appearances.

If your Press Release is a blatant sales pitch, don't expect to see it in print. Make sure your Press Release or article is newsworthy and of interest to the publication's readership. As a Press Release is not paid advertisement, it is solely up to the publisher as to whether they accept your press release for publication.

As you read this chapter, start making a list of all publications your area. Visit the publisher's website and capture the editor's name. Contact names are also found on the magazine's table of contents. Before you send out any press release, make sure the contacts are up to date. You don't want to send your press release addressed to the Editor's predecessor's name on your article or release.

While you are assessing if the publication reaches your target market group, also be on the lookout for reporters who specialize in human-interest stories. Reporters specializing in human interest stories will be more receptive to a story about you than a business reporter would. A human-interest reporter will belikely to present your idea to a publisher.

Catalog your media list in your CRM, Customer Relationship Management software system.

As you compile your media list, also note the lead time required by each publication. Lead time is the time between the date the newspaper first receives your press release, the time needed to review it, and time required before the newspaper prints your release.

Typically, newspapers require one to two weeks of lead time. For example, if you plan a grand opening on May 15, make sure your local newspaper has the press release by May 1. The newspaper may release it on the date specified or shortly thereafter. For instance, if there is no space in the news for your release on May 15, they may elect to print your press release on May 16 or 17.

The lead time for magazines is generally one to two months. National magazines require longer lead times, six to eight months or longer.

Your press release should follow standard formatting rules. In the upper-left corner of your page, state the release date in large, bold font. For example, it should read "FOR IMMEDIATE RELEASE" or if for a later date, write in "RELEASE DATE MAY 15."

On the upper-right side of the page, across from the release date, you should feature your contact information, including your name, then below your name, your phone number, with the next line your email address. This allows the editor to contact you if they have additional questions or may wish to talk to you about a feature article.

In the center of the page, compose an eye-catching headline. Be aware, editors usually like to formulate their own headlines, but if you create a clever one, they might use yours.

The first paragraph of any Press Release is the most important. Follow the five W's of journalism: who, what, when, where, and why. For example, *who* is you or your spiritual practice; *what* is you are having a grand opening; *when* is May 15; and *why* is how your practice will benefit people in your community.

Place your most important information in the first and second paragraphs. The reason for crafting it this way is if the editor chooses to trim down your press release; you have placed the most important information first.

Once your first paragraph is complete, the following paragraphs should offer additional information but be less critical to the piece. This grammatical style is organized like an inverted pyramid, with your most important information first.

In the body of your Press Release, I like to recommend one to two quotes. Quotes will make your press release more human and interesting.

Your Press Release should be no more than one to two pages. One page is best.

At the conclusion of your Press Release, repeat who, what, when, where, and why, as well as your contact number, website, and location of the event.

When your Press Release is finished, send your Press Release to newspapers, radio stations, and television stations in your area.

If the publication accepts your Press Release be sure to send the editor a thank-you note. Thank you notes are always appreciated.

Press Releases or e-press releases are not just for the media; send yours to libraries, bookstores, New Age Churches, health-food stores, and of course, add your latest Press Release to your Press Kit, offer it to customers and post your news across all your social media platforms.

Print out copies of your press release as handouts at any events you attend, and be sure to have your article on display on your website and at your store.

Publicity is not only free but one of the most cost-effective tools to strengthen your brand.

Video Press Releases

When I was in advertising, I often created video press releases for my clients. A Video Press Release is a prerecorded two to three-minute video that acts as a press release.

While you will absorb the cost of creating a video press release, if your subject is relevant and timely, you may find your video press release used as a filler on the morning news shows or featured at noon, or on the late-night news. For the most part, prime-time evening news is reserved for local news and rarely showcase human-interest stories during these peak hours.

An example of one of my video press releases was for my client who sold air conditioners. Each fall, I created a video press release on how to properly prepare home air conditioners for winter, and then each spring, I'd follow up with information on how to get the air conditioners ready for spring and summer use. This subject was timely and relevant and provided viewers with important information. It branded my client as the leader and a knowledgeable source of home and business air conditioners in my community.

For another client, I created a video press release of Halloween safety tips. The subject was timely and provided safety information for trick-or-treaters after dark and put my customer in the spotlight. Win-win.

If you have the funds, a video press release can be a good avenue to promote your practice. Be sure to also post your video press release on your YouTube Channel and website.

If you are a psychic, offer a timely insight for Valentine's Day. If you are a Medium, provide interesting information on the historical origins of Halloween. If you are a massage therapist, create an informational video on the importance of relaxation around the Christmas Holiday Season. There are any endless number of topics for you to generate new customers and information about your business.

Television advertising is very expensive, so consider a video press release.

Good luck. I hope to see everyone on the small screen.

CHAPTER 26

PROMOTIONAL ITEMS

I love Promotional Items that are clever, useful, and relative to your practice. Promotional Items support your brand and publicize your practice. However, choosing the right promotional item is crucial to this initiative being a success.

Unless you are a pizza restaurant, I'm not excited about refrigerator magnets. Besides, today most people simply have their favorite numbers programed into their phones. The same goes for pens for while personalized pens are inexpensive, after one use, they are generally tossed in the trash.

I like promotional items that have longevity, are useful and cute. Select an item that supports your practice. I personally like desk accessories that have a practical application and tend to have a long retention rate.

For my book *Lights, Camera, Murder!* I picked out miniclapboard with miniature highlighters. It says *Lights, Camera, Murder!* with my name and my website. A clapboard is the board that is used to signal the start of filming a movie scene.

For my book *Haunted Hearts,* I chose a cute little glow-in-the-dark ghost stress reliever. It says *Haunted Hearts* and my name across the front and my website on the bottom.

For my romantic comedy *Your Cheatin' Hearts,* I have a heart-shaped stress ball with the book title, my name, and my website. Stress relievers are a relatively inexpensive item, and they are also lightweight and easy to mail.

If you can find something that works for your practice, it can be a good investment. Remember as you are choosing a promotional item, consider the cost, how your item will affect and support your branding, and the return you expect to receive.

I have previously mentioned bookmarks. While inexpensive, they do have a bit of longevity. Other useful items that have a prolonged existence include but are not limited to bag clips, ice scrapers, jar openers, and keyboard dust brushes.

These items can be purchased in bulk at any office supply stores including online throughVistaPrint.com.

Promotional items are fun attention grabbers, but make sure they will work for you before you make the investment.

One-of-a-Kind Promotional Items

As you think about promoting your practice, you don't always have to purchase in bulk; you can purchase one item to promote you and your practice. For instance, when I attend a yoga class or conference, I have my personalized water bottle, which features my practice name and logo. It attracts attention, is a great conversation starter, and provides me with an opportunity to promote my practice.

I also have a customized tote, an attractive notebook with this book cover on it, and I wear shirts and hats that promote my practice. Having a personalized promotional item at an event or presentation will make you look polished and professional and is a great advertisement for your practice.

Hats are great attention grabbers, and of course, carry your items in a personalized tote, a duffle bag for the gym or personalized backpack.

You can purchase one-of-a-kind clothing options to include outerwear, shorts, T-shirts, running gear, hoodies, sweaters, computer cases, and lunch bags.

If you attend meetings and conferences, also consider a specialty name tag. I attend numerous meetings of all sizes and speak at many conferences. The meetings typically offer inexpensive badges where you are invited to write your name with a marker. You will stand out from the crowd with your own customized name tag. I have my logo and name on a plastic name tag. It looks beautiful and makes me look professional. I recommend you customize your own logo to a customized magnetic name badge, as it will make you look as polished and professional as you are.

These one-of-a-kind business promotional items will get you noticed when you are out exercising. And, of course, never leave the house without your business or networking cards.

Promotional items make your practice memorable. One-of-a-kind promotional items will help you promote your business and will inspire you and your dream.

CHAPTER 27

PUBLIC SPEAKING

Public Speaking and Personal Appearances are amazing platforms allows you to reach a lot of people in a single event.

Public Speaking gives you exposure, strengthens your brand, and offers the opportunity to make a personal connection with everyone in attendance. The publicity you can garner around your appearance allows you to publicize your practice before and after the event. If you film your presentation, you can post it online and feature it on your website. Public Speaking is the gift that keeps on giving as your video presentation is shared with new viewers.

I've been doing public speaking for so long, it's second nature to me now. I acquired this skill through hours of practice and many speaking opportunities. Public speaking is an acquired skill that is earned over time.

Imagining someone scantily clad in the audience might bring a polite smile to your face, but it won't help you overcome the jitters or make your delivery smoother. Practice will. Practice in front of friends. Practice in front of family. Practice in front of your kids and your pets; at least your pets will continue to show adoration after the third time. Practice until your speech is perfect and until you are able to deliver it with ease. Practice in front of a mirror; watch your mannerisms and smile!

Begin your presentation with a hook. A hook is those first few sentences in a novel or the first moments of a television show that captures and intrigues the audience.

Next, develop three to five key points on your topic and structure your lecture around them. As you are developing your presentation, ask yourself what are the most important points about your talk that will be interesting and make an impression about your practice. As you develop your talk, stay within time limits offered for your speech.

Interject personal stories or experiences, but never use real names unless you have their permission to do so. Wherever possible, add a touch of humor.

Close with a satisfying ending and leave time for questions. Conclude your presentation with a call to action to schedule appointments and a bit of lighthearted self-promotion.

Use visual aids. Visual aids will not only keep you on track but will keep your audience focused on your speech.

If you have invested in a retractable sign or banner or backdrop to your presentation, be sure to bring it with you.

Larger venues, such as libraries and lecture halls, typically, they will have an array of audio equipment available. If none is available, you may want to consider purchasing your own video or audio equipment or even renting audio equipment for such occasions. If you feel you want to continue to pursue speaking engagements, consider purchasing your own equipment. You can also rent equipment; look under rent audio equipment in your town.

Bring a door prize to raffle off to members attending, and bring your appointment book to schedule appointments. Offer a small gift to the group's coordinator or the person who helped in scheduling your presentation, and make sure to have a thank-you card ready as you leave for the group's coordinator.

If you are ready to tackle this promotional opportunity, identify groups and organizations in your area. If you find a good fit, contact the group's coordinator, introduce yourself and your practice. Present your idea. Remember, it's the coordinator's job to find interesting speakers at their events, so don't be shy about making that phone call to a group.

The program coordinator may request more information about you. If they do, send your media kit or Tip Sheet, along with any reviews you have collected from previous speaking engagements.

If they agree to schedule your presentation to the group, make sure you understand your allotted time and know how many people typically attend, especially if you plan on bringing handouts or flyers. Bring extra copies for a larger-than-average turnout.

As you solidify your speaking engagement, ask what sort of publicity the group offers, and tell them of publicity you are planning for your engagement.

The day of your presentation, do not trust your moderator to introduce you properly. Write down your own introduction, and upon arrival, slip it to your moderator. Bring two copies. The first one you hand to the moderator upon arrival; then have a second introduction handy, in case the coordinator misplaces the first introduction.

Remember, when giving a talk, be yourself, relax, and smile. The audience has come to see and hear what you have to say.

During your presentation, make eye contact with the audience. Remember to smile. Smile. Smile. Smile. Body language is important, so appear relaxed, even if you are not. Speak from the heart, and speak with passion. Be excited and animated. If you make a blunder in the middle of the talk or lose your place, it's okay; it happens. Once in the middle of a lecture to a writer's group, I became so engaged with a series of questions, I lost my place. I told the group so, and they laughed with me. We moved on, no harm, no foul. Humility makes you human.

If someone leaves during your talk, don't be offended, as it could be an emergency or other valid reason they must leave. Focus on the people in the room who are not leaving.

Here are some additional tips.

Arrive thirty minutes ahead of time. Don't count on audio or video equipment or even the room to be set up and ready for you. You may have to take care of that yourself.

If you have handouts such as your business cards, flyers, or brochures, have them available at the registration table.

I bring a prepared review form and ask for the audience to share their thoughts on my presentation. I add the reviews I collect in my book of reviews and on my website. I only use first name, last initial when posting my reviews, as well as the date and place of my presentation.

There are a limitless number of public speaking opportunities in your area, including civic and women's groups, writers' and Meet-up groups, and organizations through your community. You would be especially welcome at New Age churches and events.

Not all public appearances and speaking engagements need to be in front of a large crowd. Small groups are also looking for speakers. Fairies would be a great subject for a garden group, and everyone is interested in Angels.

Reach out to local hotels that have business and trade conferences at their locations. Hotel sales managers are always looking for interesting presentations to offer their guests.

Are there Campgrounds nearby your home or a national or regional park? Rangers will welcome your presentation about wild herbs, astrology, and local legends at special park events and festivals. If you are speaking to these groups, make sure your items for sale are made available at any campground stores.

Think outside of the box when it comes to promoting yourself and your spiritual practice through public speaking engagements.

If you relatively new to public speaking, you can improve your presentation skills by becoming a member of your local Toastmasters group. Toastmasters is a group of nice folks who will help you improve your public speaking and communication skills and help you build your confidence.

While your original intent is to promote your practice, you may find yourself sought after by businesses and corporations, as corporate America is always on the lookout for motivational speakers.

Public Speaking is a great way to become known and establish yourself as an expert in your field. Your dynamic presentation can expand into additional public speaking opportunities.

Public Speaking gives you credibility, supports brand awareness, will heighten recognition, and best of all, creates and strengthens word-of-mouth recommendations about your practice.

See you at the podium. I'll be in your front row cheering!

CHAPTER 28

RADIO FM, AM, AND INTERNET

We love Radio! We listen to radio at the gym, in our homes, on the internet, in our vehicles, and at the workplace. The average American owns three radios, and a whopping 93 percent of Americans still turn to radio for news and entertainment.

Whether you are listening to AM, FM or Internet Radio; radio offers you a powerful medium to promote your spiritual practice.

AM and FM Radio

When considering radio, begin by identifying radio stations you feel would be most receptive to your message. AM stations, for the most part, offer a local talk format. Most FM talk shows and Online Radio stations offer listeners nationally syndicated music, sports, political genres, and news.

FM is more expensive than AM, and while their weekday schedules are filled with nationally syndicated shows, you might be able to identify locally produced show times that are available on the weekend.

Before purchasing advertising on any radio station, take time to listen to the station; know the audience and the on-air personalities. Once you have a good grasp of their market, you can assess if the station's format would work for you. Avoid shock jocks and those who practice "got ya" interviews and make their living ridiculing and embarrassing their guests.

Radio stations typically post their media kits on their website. The station's media kit gives you information on their format, their listeners; make sure their listeners are a good match for your target market. Be knowledgeable about the station's format and hosts before you place your call.

When you reach the receptionist, ask for the person who is in charge of booking guests. You will likely be turned over to the station's producer, or if it's a small station, be sent directly to the host. Use your elevator pitch to introduce yourself and state why you would be of interest to their listeners.

Being a local Medium, Clairvoyant, or Herbalist might in and of itself be enough to land you a guest spot on a radio show. The radio producer will say yes, no, or request more information about you or your subject.

Send them your Press Kit or your Tip Sheet, and prepare a list of suggested questions with your answers for the interview. Do be prepared for additional questions the host might ask.

Throughout the year, at scheduled intervals, touch base with the producers to discuss seasonal topics of interest. For instance, in October remind the station's programing director you are available to talk about witches, magic, and mediumship on Halloween. In February, suggest a conversation about love and romance. Bill your brand as America's or your town's favorite psychic, and let that be part of your branding.

If you are invited to be a guest speaker on a station, role play with a friend and make sure you are comfortable when sitting in front of a microphone.

As suggested, before your interview, send in you're a suggested list of questions with your answers, along with your introduction.

During the show itself, focus on the radio host, and present yourself as polished, friendly, and professional. Speak clearly. Smile. Listeners can't see you, but they can hear your smile. They can also hear any throat lozenges or gum in your mouth. Keep your message on point, and make sure mention how listeners can get in touch with you.

Make your Radio Host shine, and you'll be invited back.

When your appearance is over, ask for a copy of the tape of the show, and send a thank-you note to everyone who helped you with your radio appearance.

Don't wait for the station to call you back; take the initiative and offer fresh topics every quarter.

Internet Radio

Internet Radio offers a world of rich opportunities, especially with many New Age talk shows already on the web. Hosts are always on the lookout for new and interesting guests.

Whether online or in the real world, the same rules apply. Listen to radio stations, and understand the station's audience to identify stations that would be receptive to your message. Contact the host to explore opportunities with them as a featured guest, and if you are invited, send your Media Kit or Tip Sheet, along with suggested questions for the host.

The majority of internet radio interviews will be conducted over the telephone. During your interview, turn off your cell phones, radios, and television and keep children and pets quiet.

Be focused on the host. Have a glass of water handy in case your throat goes dry. As I stated earlier, don't have candy, cough drops, or gum in your mouth, as the microphone will pick up those ever-so-faint sounds.

Like AM/FM Radio, Internet radio offers the same variety of talk, news, sports, and music. Generally, there is no charge for an on-air appearance; however, some internet radio shows will charge you an appearance fee. If you have to pay for an appearance, make sure the investment will be worth the exposure.

Hosting Your Own Radio Show

Before I conclude this chapter, I'd like to mention another opportunity in radio, and that is, hosting your own New Age radio show. Most talk stations feature nationally syndicated radio talk shows during the week, however, there may be an opportunity to showcase your practice during weekend programing.

Be on the lookout for stations that offer local programing. Local programing includes local gardening and real-estate shows, and shows about auto and home repair. Spend time listening to weekend radio shows as you consider this option before you fully commit to this marketing initiative.

If you feel you would like to host your own radio show, meet with the station's account executive, and find out if time is available for a thirty to sixty-minute talk show. If time is available, create a series of topics for a six-week programing schedule. Understand how to break the show and topics into segments around station commercial breaks. I would suggest you have a minimum of six show idea, to start, revolving around your spiritual practice.

If the time is available, the radio station will expect you to pay up front for your programs, as well as all costs associated with your show. This includes technical assistance during the show.

You can offset the cost of your radio show by selling commercial time to advertisers. Look for advertisers in your Meet-up groups, as well as companies you buy from. For instance, do you use a cleaning service? Contact the cleaning service or anyone who does business with you, and offer them a commercial in your show.

If you are a yoga instructor or personal trainer who works at a gym; invite the fitness center to advertise on your show. If your radio show is about healthy eating, contact local growers and grocery stores, as you are also reaching their target market.

New Age book stores might be interested in your market, as well as restaurants that offer vegetarian or vegan options. Soliciting advertisers will offset the cost of the show and make it an affordable marketing initiative.

Typically, in an hour show there are four significant commercial breaks where you can offer two to three minutes of commercials. These commercial breaks usually occur at the quarter hours and the half hour. Offer your advertisers thirty-second to sixty-second commercials.

Offsetting the costs of your show though commercials is one aspect of this investment, finding a sponsor is another.

It is important to be comfortable in presenting your radio show, and this includes speaking in front of a microphone as well as understanding the signals given to you by technicians and engineers.

If you show becomes popular and outgrows your local market, consider syndication. Your station's account executive will be able to help you get your show picked up by other stations across the country.

If your goal is to reach a worldwide market, consider an Internet Radio show or a Podcast. Creating your own radio show can be ambitious undertaking, understanding but it can result in not only gaining new clients for your practice but raising your profile in your community.

CHAPTER 29

TELEVISION

Seeing an ad about your practice on television can be both intoxicating and exhilarating. Thirty- to sixty-second television ads are expensive. In addition to paying for airtime, you will also have to absorb all production costs.

If you feel you would like to explore this advertising on the small screen, look at the station's Media Kit and schedule an appointment with the station's sales department to discuss the opportunities available to you.

As you look at the station's demographics. Understand what viewers are watching, when they are watching as well as the cost and charge to produce your commercial.

Rates will be higher during the daytime and prime time. Prime time occurs between the national evening news to late night news. After midnight, advertising rates are lower, but keep in mind fewer people are watching.

You can offset the production costs of your television advertisement by working with a small video production house.

I have placed many clients on television, both in the national and regional markets, however, as a whole, due to the high costs, I don't recommend it for the small spiritual practice.

A one-time ad is not going to garner you a great response, as your ad will only reach people who are watching at that exact time. To have any kind of response, you will have to run your commercial multiple times. This is called *Frequency.*

While you will reach a lot of viewers on television, ask yourself how many of those viewers will actually view your ad, retain your message, and of course be subsequently prompted to pick up the phone and schedule an appointment.

If you feel you still want to promote yourself on television, meet with a station's account executive and review opportunities that could work for you. For instance, if the station is aware of any upcoming shows featuring New Age Personalities, you might be able to place a one-time commercial on Dr. Phil or Dr. Oz's show, if their shows feature a well-known medium or expert in your field.

There are other opportunities on television.

Public Relations Opportunities in Television

While television ads may be cost prohibitive, don't be discouraged; television does offer you other opportunities that could work in your favor.

Television producers, editors, and reporters are always on the lookout for human-interest stories. Stations like to air human-interest stories of local events and captivating individuals who shape their community. Human-interest stories typically are aired on local morning, noon, and sometime late-evening news segments.

As you watch your local TV, look for reporters who cover human-interest stories. Reach out to these reporters, and invite them to do a story about you. Before you call, have your idea ready. You will find reporters' contact information on the station's website.

Whether you decide to directly contact the human-interest reporter, the editorial staff, or producer, I recommend you develop a story idea and have an explanation ready as to why your story would be of interest to their viewers. Your idea should be timely, relevant, and of interest to the station's audience.

Don't be discouraged if they initially decline your first offering; leave a positive impression, and advise the decision maker to consider you a local resource for trending national stories. Send a thank-you note and your media kit or tip sheet to the station.

In television, timing is everything. The Christmas Holidays are a good time to talk about Angels or how yoga can help reduce stress during the holiday season. Halloween might be the time of year for a story on Mediumship. Valentine's Day is a perfect time to offer a psychic consultation on romance. If something is happening in the sky or by a moon phase, advise the station your expertise in how the planetary changes can affect the human psyche.

While you are speaking to the station, be sure to take advantage of the moment and establish yourself as an expert. Many stations will keep names and phone numbers of local experts for news stories. You never know when a story about angels, crystals, or mediumship might suddenly trend on popular media.

Be aware that human-interest story might be bumped, rescheduled, or even canceled if breaking news occurs during your segment.

Post any appearances on all your social media, and if your segment was canceled, post that too.

Television is a visual medium, so look your best. Take care of your appearance, your makeup, and your wardrobe. Wear solids, as stripes and heavy patterns will look busy on screen. Keep your hand gestures to a minimum.

If this is your first interview, don't let the viewers know it. Practice with a friend or associate, as practice makes perfect. Be sure you make a copy of your interview for your website and video platforms.

PSA and Television Community Calendars

In addition to commercials, television and radio stations both offer Public Service Announcements are referred to as PSAs. PSAs are designed to inform and educate the general public. Advertising is paid; Public Service Announcements are free. An example of a Public Service Announcement is law enforcement reminding the public not to drink and drive.

If you have a free and or educational event that is open to the public, consider sending a PSA to the Public Service Director at your local television or radio station. Your PSA might be featured as a standalone announcement or featured in the community calendar.

Your grand opening will not, in and of itself, be considered a public service announcement, but your speaking engagement at a local library might make the television station's community calendar.

Several years back, I enjoyed being featured on the local television station's community calendar. The announcement ran for thirty days and gave me a tremendous amount of publicity. The PSA read "Local Author Linn Random will be the featured speaker Saturdays from 1 till 3 at the local library. The event is free, the public is invited to learn about how to write the great American novel." Thousands were exposed to the event, and the mention itself garnered an upswing in local book sales.

If you are involved in a charity event, send your notice to the Public Service director for inclusion in the community calendar. If you create a PSA, make sure the charity is the center of attention. Don't worry, I assure you, your name will get noticed.

Television commercials can cost thousands of dollars to make and broadcast. Public Service Announcements are free and will not only boost your credibility but build trust and increase your bottom line.

CHAPTER 30

THEATER AND MOVIE ADVERTISING OPPORTUNITIES

Unless you are in New York City, advertising on Broadway may not be a good fit for your budget; however, your local community theater might be a nice fit if their audience sits within your target market group.

Community theaters offer live performances and are generally comprised by a small army of volunteers who are always on the lookout to raise funds for their productions. They raise funds through advertising and sponsorship opportunities.

Partnering with a Community theater will get you exposure and generate a healthy dose of good publicity. If you decide to consider this opportunity, make sure your partnership reaches your target market. Examine the costs of sponsorship, and have a clear understanding of your return on investment before you become a patron. If the numbers are comfortable for you and your budget, consider the advertising opportunities available.

Reach out to the theater's marketing coordinator to explore opportunities in the theater's program or newsletter. Ad sizes range from a business-card size to the inside front or back program cover. They might be more affordable than you think.

Other opportunities include advertising or having your name and tag line on a flyer or postcard promoting the event or sidewalk signage.

To find out about promotional opportunities available to you, simply call your local community theater. As always, advertising, marketing, and public-relations initiatives are only good if they reach your target market and bring in clients to your practice.

The Movies

Americans love the movies. In fact, over 750 million of us go to movie theaters each year. Businesses have been advertising in movie theaters since the turn of the 20th century, and there are opportunities at your local cinema for the small business, especially during the movie's preshow.

Preshow advertising is the slide show that runs on a twenty to twenty-five-minute repeating loop before the movie. The preshow features coming attractions and is designed to entertain movie patrons who arrive early. During this time, the theater will advise moviegoers to turn off their cell phones. This leaves the audience with little to do but enjoy popcorn and focus on advertisement during the preshow.

Individual ads run fifteen to thirty seconds. Advertisers can choose a single, static image for their entire commercial or run several slides about their business. I recommend ads that engage the audience by asking trivia questions, followed by the answer on the next slide. In best-case scenarios, these should be tied to the advertiser's business.

Be on the lookout for blockbusters whose storyline resonates with your practice. Stay away from murder, mayhem, and any storyline that you would not want to be associated.

Other opportunities at your local theater include lobby signage, banners, and point of purchase counter cards.

Major advertisers with deep pockets often offer moviegoers exit samples and handouts. While this might be a nice add-on to your promotion budget, it's generally just too costly for the small spiritual practice.

Some theaters offer summer movie festivals with discounts to seniors and children. Ask if your local theater offers special summer movie presentations that would fit into your market and your budget.

Moviegoers generally live within a ten-mile radius of the theater and for the most part range in age between ages of sixteen and forty-four. Is this your market? Do upcoming films tie into your practice or industry?

If you want to consider this medium, be aware that some theater chains may request advertisers commit to a four-week run and at a specific number of theaters.

Regional theaters or a local movie theater will be less expensive. Before investing in this initiative, I would advise contacting a current advertiser to learn of their response before you invest in this opportunity. There are benefits in advertising at the movies, but be sure it makes sense to you. This advertising medium is only good if it brings in customers. Depending on your region of the country, it can be costly, so you may decide to save your advertising dollars for more affordable endeavors. However, if the movie is right and you feel it could benefit you, I'll see you at the movies!

CHAPTER 31

CONCLUSION— REAL-WORLD MARKETING

There are unlimited possibilities to promote your practice in the real world. These opportunities will yield financial rewards, especially in local and regional markets. Real-world promotional strategies will drive traffic to your location, increase sales, and promote your practice. Even if your business is online, don't overlook local promotional opportunities that could bring you revenue.

Real-world promotional strategies will not only highlight your presence but underscore your credibility and extend your reach on the web.

In the next section, I'll be offering promotional strategies on the web. In the meantime, review sections in real-world marketing strategies for inclusion in your Marketing Plan, which will be featured in the last section of this book.

You don't have to take advantage of every single opportunity presented in this section, but do take advantage of those you that suit you and your budget.

Good luck with your Real-World marketing strategies. You can always write me with your questions on my blog, www.*TheBusinessSide. blog*.

In the next section, we will look at promotional opportunities on the World Wide Web.

PART III

MARKETING ON THE WORLD WIDE WEB

The world is your oyster on the web. This section will give you an overview on online marketing strategies. As the marketing opportunities on the internet continue to grow, I will be posting new ideas and concepts on my blog, *TheBusinessSide.blog*, as well as inviting you to share new ideas. For now, let's look at opportunities online that are currently available to you.

CHAPTER 32

BLOGGING

A Blog is an online platform for personal and business use. Many businesses use their Blog site as their primary website.

I'd like to share with you a quick snapshot of the evolution of blogs. In the early days, bloggers were mostly comprised of new Moms and individuals who shared lifestyle strategies from weight loss to fashion. Authors entered the world of blogging and used blogs to connect with readers, promote their books, and shared their writing life.

Educators came on board and used their blogs to connect with students and provide them with course study material.

Today, blogs promote all types of businesses as well as providing insights on sports, entertainment, and political opinions. If you have an interest or hobby, I can assure you, you can find a blog about it, hundreds of them.

The goal of your blog is to solidify your customer base and attract new clients. In addition, your blog will help promote your practice, establish you as an industry leader, as well as showcase contests and your promotional events.

Begin your blog by securing a domain name. Use the name of your spiritual practice or your name.

Be aware a blog is labor intensive, and you need to calculate the amount of time you spend working on your blog vs. the number of new customers you expect to gain. Time is Money, so when calculating and understanding this, spend your time as wisely as you do your money.

If you are new to blogging, take the time to understand how a blog works. Find a blog that interests you, and enjoy reading it as you begin to formulate ideas for your own blog.

When you are ready to start your blog, your options are a choice of a free service or purchasing from a premium blogging site. Register your blog at GoDaddy.com, WordPress.com, or a blog hosting site of your choosing. Both GoDaddy.com and WordPress.com will walk you through the how-to of creating a blog and adding content to it.

Make your blog posts as formal or informal as you wish. I'd recommend you be friendly, respectful, and informative. Select an easy-to-read font. Don't clutter your blog pages with ads or in any way make them too busy with graphics. Your content will get lost in advertisements and photos, so keep both to a minimum. Keep the colors, font, and image consistent with your brand.

Create a monthly theme that directly ties into your practice. People read blogs for education, information, and to be entertained, so stay away from controversy, as it will offend half your readers.

Some bloggers post three times a week. Others post once a week. Decide what works best for you. I'm in the middle and like two blogs per week. If you post three blogs, say one on Monday, a second on Wednesday, it is my belief the third time you blog appears on Friday, it might become lost in weekend plans and activities. Keep your blog relevant, and don't bombard your users' emails.

Your blog post should be a minimum of two hundred to three hundred words, which is about the word count of a single page. As I write this, there is a new trend among bloggers to create posts upwards of up to sixteen hundred words, which is roughly seven pages. This length depends on your subject, topic, and how you frame your blog. I maintain that less is more, as you want your readers to find your posts fresh, interesting, quick to read, and rich with information. You decide what works best for you. I, however, urge you to be and stay consistent as you deliver your content to your readers on a time and on schedule.

Blogs are read in reverse chronological order, which means the newest will be read first. So, if you post on Monday and then follow with a second blog on Wednesday, your Wednesday blog will be read first by someone visiting your site. Your Monday post will appear below the Wednesday post.

Use your blog to educate your readers about your practice and inform them about your services and products. Don't make every blog post a blatant sales promotion. That said, it's perfectly acceptable to offer the occasional special, discount, or contest available to your blog readers.

Engage and interact with your readers by asking open-ended questions. Invite readers to share their thoughts, opinions, and experiences. Making your blog an open forum will give your readers a sense of community and a connection to you.

I recommend also inviting guest bloggers to post on your blog. Guest bloggers add variety to your blog as well as bring their followers to your blog site. And of course, hosting a guest blogger on your site gives you the opportunity to promote your blog.

Make your blog appealing and your content interesting and relative to your practice and registration for your blog easy.

Some bloggers have turned their blogs into an additional revenue streams by making money through banners, advertising, and affiliate marketing. Keep in mind, before those additional dollars come in, you need have the web traffic on your blog before the advertisers will make an ad purchase. You drive visitors to your blog by promoting your blog site across all your social media platforms. Remember, your primary goal for your blog is to have new customers schedule appointments with you. Be realistic and know it will take time and commitment to build your blog readership.

Make sure your blog offers a safe place to learn about your practice and industry. Allow your customers to connect to each other and to you. Don't be shy in removing someone who is rude, abrasive, or negative to you or others.

If your blog is comprised of local or regional readers and customers, consider inviting your them to an afternoon tea at your store or watch party.

You might entertain turning your blog into a regular column in your local New Age newspaper or offer it as a syndicated column for newspaper in the real world or online.

Promote your blog on your business or networking card, your electronic business card, and signature line. Mention your blog when you speak or at events you attend.

Your blog should a mix of information and education. Your readers should see value. Keep your blog entertaining.

If you like the idea of blogging but feel it may take more time than you are willing to dedicate to it, you may find vlogs or video blogs more suited to you, and of course, you are invited to my blog, which will be an ongoing source of marketing information as I inform you of marketing concepts and new trends on my blog. *TheBusinessSide.blog.*

Video Blogging—The Vlog

Vlogs are video blogs. Instead of writing a blog, you can sit in front of a video camera and simply chat about your topic of the week or month.

Vlogging visually connects you with viewers. YouTube users will be able to add comments and thoughts and subscribe to your network.

Review the chapter on Online Classes for tips on how to present yourself in front of a camera.

Popular vlogs run somewhere between ninety seconds and three minutes. Be sure you invite viewers to like your video, subscribe to your channel, and of course, encourage viewers to your website.

If you sell herbs or aromatherapy, talk about how these practices can benefit practitioners. If you are a card reader, show how you do a card reading or offer a card reading each week or month. Yoga instructors are making a name for themselves by showcasing a series of poses to benefit the shoulders, back, or other areas.

Plan monthly themes and record them in your promotional calendar. You will find more information about how to create a marketing and promotional calendar in Part IV of this book.

Vlogging is a great way for your customers to see you and become comfortable with you. Customers will connect with you.

In Conclusion

Blogging can be labor intensive. If your time is limited, you might want to stay in touch with your customers via a newsletter or through an email marketing campaign.

Whether you are blogging or vlogging, this is a promotional strategy that will expand your customer base, build trust, create loyalty, and increase your bottom line.

In the next chapter, I will share more information about chat rooms and videoconferencing.

CHAPTER 33

CHAT ROOMS AND VIDEO CONFERENCING

Chat Rooms are virtual communities where people around the world discuss interests and share knowledge. Chat room users have the opportunity to chat and interact with others in real time. Some chat rooms are free; others charge users to participate.

To find a New Age Chat room, conduct an internet search. You will find hundreds of New Age chat rooms with subjects ranging from horoscopes to Angels, yoga, mediums, and psychics, and so much more. If you have an interest in a subject, I assure you, there is a chat room to support it.

A hundred years ago, or so it seems to me now, I used to participate in author chats on book review sites. I paid for the opportunity to chat about my books. The chat consisted of an instant messaging platform where my guests asked me questions and I responded. There was a moderator who assisted me throughout the chat. At the end of each chat, I'd have a drawing among attendees for a special prize giveaway. It was a great opportunity to promote my books.

Today, chat technology has moved from instant messaging to live video presentations.

When considering hosting a chat, I first recommend you participate as a visitor in a video chat, so you can understand how chat rooms function and flow.

You can host your own chat on your website or through a simple, easy-to-access forum such as Facebook Live.

However, you decide to host your chat, prepare a cheat sheet to help you stay on point, as well as any documents you may wish to cut and paste into your presentation to illustrate a point within your presentation. This is a perfect application for your High Concept and Tip Sheet.

Make registration for your chat easy, and of course promote your chat across all your social media outlets. Promote your chat several days and weeks in advance, hours, and minutes before your chat, and during.

Don't be discouraged if only six people will show up for a chat; hundreds will have read your promotional announcements before and after your chat. Promoting your chat is worth its weight in publicity gold.

Video Conferencing

Many companies now rely videoconferencing to conduct business, as it allows people from anywhere in the world to communicate in a live setting.

Video chats or conference calls thrive on an instant messaging platform such as FaceTime, Google Hangouts, Skype, GoToMeeting, and Zoom, to mention just a few video conferencing platforms. Video Conferencing is a good way to communicate and interact with your clients.

Whether you are offering a private one on one psychic consultation or a group reading, videoconferencing is an easy way to communicate with people, as attendees can participate via their desktop computers, mobile phones, iPads, or tablets and they can talk to you from their home, at the gym, or on their lunch break.

If you are new to conducting an online chat, host a practice chat with a few friends. Test your equipment for sound, for lighting, and for staging.

I once attended an online chat where I had to wait almost fifteen minutes while the hostess adjusted the camera and microphone. It was awkward and uncomfortable for her, and I am sure other attendees, like myself, were wondering why we had set aside time to attend this chat. First impressions count, so respect your time and the time of your guests.

Keep your background uncluttered and your presentation area clean and simple. No dirty dishes in the sink or family photos to take away the focus from you. Turn off any cell phones whose ring could interrupt your conference.

Dress appropriately; business casual is perfect. Leave the fairy wings, Renaissance clothing, and exotic decorations for another time. You want to be comfortable and present yourself as the talented professional you are.

Keep your hand movements and eye movements to a minimum. Remember to smile as you speak.

If you use music, keep it soft, so as not to overpower your presentation.

As you address your attendees, keep your voice natural. Don't shout into the camera. If your attendees cannot hear you, they can adjust the volume on their devices. Eliminate background noises, and tell your household you need quiet for your live presentation.

Look directly at the camera. The camera should be at eye level, not too high, as you don't want to look down at your customers, or too low, as you don't want to have your customers looking down at you. Position your camera eye level. I'd like to suggest you purchase camera tripod. You can find tripods under twenty dollars, and they are worth the investment.

Videoconferencing can be conducted one on one, in group settings, on a regular monthly or quarterly basis. They are fun and will promote your business around the globe, bringing in new customers and clients.

If you host a video chat, promote your chat across all social media platforms and be sure to mention your chat at all personal appearances.

CHAPTER 34

EMAIL MARKETING

One of the simplest and most effective marketing strategies is through email marketing. An email campaign strengthens your bond with your clients, increases customer loyalty, encourages repeat business, and converts prospects into customers.

Your prime objective in every marketing initiative is to capture and collect the email addresses. By doing so, you will build and solidify your customer base and convert prospects into paying customers.

Your email is a lifeline between you and your customers. Sending out your newsletters, contests, notices, and special promotions to your base will keep you top of mind. Top of mind means when customers consider turning to a psychic or practitioner in your field, they will think of you first.

Make sure you have your recipient's permission before you send out your email, as you want it to appear in their inbox, not delegated to their spam folder.

The best way to create your email list is to do it organically over time. Let it grow naturally. Build your customer email base through newsletters, contests and events, and public speaking opportunities. Be sure you mention "by registering for a prize, your newsletter, or blog," the registrant consents to receive emails and promotions from you. Also add that all information you collect will not be sold or shared with any third party.

As a whole, I do not recommend buying email lists. Buying an email list can be a slippery slope. While you can buy email lists, I have found purchased email mailing lists for the most part wind up in spam folders, never to be read or viewed by the recipient.

There are always exceptions to the rule. For example, if you are a yoga instructor, you might want to contact a yoga magazine, to see if their subscribers list is obtainable for your area. This list might also be available through a direct mail house. If you find such a list, for best results, purchase your target markets' zip codes in your area.

If you offer crystals, send out a monthly email about a particular crystal. Make your emails relevant to the season and a reason to visit or schedule an appointment with you.

When you send out emails, give thought to your subject line, and create an interesting or provocative title that begs to be open and read.

The email message should be topical, educational, and of value and importance, relevant to the reader, and close with a call to action. A call to action is designed to evoke an immediate response to your email post. For example, to "Call Now for an appointment" or "Offer Expires May 15" or "Place your order now for special pricing."

If you have your clients' birthdays, send out a birthday greeting along with a special discount, and use emails stay in touch all year with holiday greetings from New Year's to Valentine's Day to Christmas Holidays. If you have your customers' physical addresses, send out a holiday postcards. Keep track of clients' birthdays and emails in your CRM system to send out individual or group emails. You can also print out postal labels from most CRMs.

If you participated in an event, send out email thank-you notes to everyone who stopped by your booth or shared their email with you.

Periodically send out thank-you cards or emails thanking customers for their business. Everyone like to feel appreciated, so let each customer know they are valued.

Back in the 1980s, I watched a launch from Kennedy Space Center. As I watched the Space Shuttle rise into the heavens, I formulated a letter for my hotel client to send to the various companies that had contributed to that launch. One CEO of a major aerospace corporation, who had taken part in the space program for decades, wrote my client, stating it was the first time anyone in the local community had acknowledged his company's participation in the space program. My client enjoyed thousands of dollars in hotel bookings from a single thank-you letter. Everyone wants to be valued and appreciated.

Don't continuously offer discounts in every email you send, as customers will become accustomed to receiving these discount offers and will wait until your next markdown. Customers who pay attention to bargain-basement pricing will become reluctant to pay full price. Don't devalue your services. Save your discounts for new customers, current clients who haven't been in a while and, as suggested, once or possibly twice a year as an incentive.

Your emails should be a trusted source of reliable information, education, and a place to promote your monthly contests.

Remember that the bulk of your customers are using their cell phones to view messages, so size matters. Lengthy emails will be hard to read on a small screen. Your email should be in an easy-to-read format.

One last word about emails: get a business email. Sending a business email from, for example, LinnRandom@TheBusinessSide.com is more professional than using a Gmail or Yahoo account.

A good email marketing campaign sent out at appropriate intervals will create brand loyalty with your customers and keep them coming back for more!

CHAPTER 35

FACEBOOK

Facebook is one of the largest social media networking platforms on the internet. Whether you are connecting with your customers on FaceTime, hosting a live event, or just interacting on your Facebook, Facebook will likely play a prominent role of your online social media marketing platforms.

Facebook was created by Mark Zuckerberg when he was enrolled at Harvard University. The original concept was to provide a platform where students could connect with one another. The concept proved so popular, it leapfrogged from the Harvard Campus to encompass the world.

Facebook offers users a platform to share their lives, share restaurant meals, scenic locations, and social causes they believe in. My favorite is an unending collection of puppy videos. Just about everyone has a Facebook page.

Facebook users access their Facebook page from computers, tablets, laptops, and mobile phones. On Facebook, you have a choice between creating a business page or a personal page. If you'd like to join Facebook, you will first be asked to create a login. If you are using your Facebook Page as your primary business page, pay attention to your profile photos, colors, and the visual images you share.

Post regularly; post events and promotions. Interact and engage with those who respond to your posts, as you are creating a business community of friends and customers.

Don't rely on your users to keep your group members entertained; post questions and solicit comments and opinions to keep your group active. Photos and videos will capture more attention than just simple posts. You can create links to your blogs and other social media platforms, and be sure to include your Facebook link to each platform.

Creating your own group will build loyalty and interest in you but help you establish a community that encourages both new and repeat business.

Facebook is a great place to announce sales, special promotions, and events, and whenever possible tie them into news that is trending. For instance, if a royal or celebrity wedding is in your news feed of the day, offer special royal or astrological insights and charts for your customers. Take advantage of any major news story that is relevant to your practice.

Monitor your Facebook page for rude or unseemly behavior. Remove these people, block them, and bless them on their upward journeys.

Keep your political opinions to yourself and off all social media platforms. There is no faster way to alienate your half of your customers than voicing an opposing political view. Sadly, I had to remove a dear friend because of hate-filled political rants. There are plenty of sites that allow people to express their opinions, I strongly recommend you stay away from such discussions on your site, as you are guaranteed to offend those who hold different political views. And while I am at it, I was so relieved to read the owner of one of my favorite Facebook groups stated there was to be no political opinions on her site. This was wonderful, I thought, until two days later, I read her hate-filled post on another site, using her practice name. As I live in a no-hate zone, I left both sites. I support everyone's right to free speech; publishing your political opinions in a public forum could cause you to lose half of your customer base.

It's okay to root for your home sports team and have a bit of fun with it. It's okay to share your passions about life. Be human as you practice the divine. Stay on point with positive messages; your customers and your growing bank account will appreciate it.

Posting National Days is a great way to keep your contacts engaged. You can find an endless list of National Days in a simple internet search, and they are super fun! For instance, May 23 is National Lucky Penny Day, a perfect occasion to post an affirmation on abundance. August 22 is National Be an Angel Day, ideal for mentioning angels or inviting your members to share Angel encounters. If you offer massage therapy, don't miss Everyone Deserves a Massage Week. If you offer healing herbs, mention it on Herbs and Spice Day, June 10. Each day of the year offers a national day to celebrate and might work in your favor for fun and profit.

National Days are a great way to have your contacts keep in touch with you and keep your practice top of mind each day of the year. You can find an endless list of promotional opportunities by doing an internet search for National Days.

Be sure to notice birthdays and anniversaries among your Facebook group. I mention the next statement in both my sales and writing classes; people will never care about you until you show that you care about them.

Here are some quick tips to get noticed on Facebook and gain followers.

1. Create an interesting Facebook page with dazzling photos and pictures.
2. Encourage friends and followers to share your posts.
3. Encourage friends and followers to like your posts.
4. Tag friends and get yourself tagged by friends and customers.
5. Be sure to notice and engage with your followers.
6. Post Positive Messages, and keep those messages short. Complicated, long posts don't get read or shared. Make your posts upbeat and easy to read and digest.
7. Have your customers leave a review; encourage them to do so by offering them a one-time discount or free reading.
8. Post a contest or giveaway or occasional special discount.
9. Post video content and links to your YouTube channel and other social media platforms.
10. Keep your conversation going with interesting conversation starters that encourage responses.
11. Offer a promotion day for your members.
12. Create a Facebook Group.
13. Tap into local, regional, and world news events that tie into your practice.
14. Go live through a Facebook Live event.

15. Make your Facebook page a location that visitors and followers visit daily.

16. Find and share vivid posts that tie into your practice.

As you work in the Facebook environment, remember your Facebook page is about your practice, so stay on point. We are going to continue exploring Facebook marketing opportunities in the following subsections.

Facebook Groups

You can create your own Facebook Group from your Facebook home page. The process is easy; just click on *group* from your Facebook home page and follow the prompts.

You will be able to set rules, select the privacy setting you wish, and make your group open, closed, or by invitation only.

Keep close tabs on notifications and posts within your group. Encourage your followers to engage and communicate with each other. Invite local Facebook friends to events at your store or to a speaking appearance. Promote your Facebook group on your website and on all your social media outlets.

I recommend growing your group organically; by growing it naturally, you are able to create a community of people who support you and your mission.

Facebook groups are popular and I urge you to consider creating a Facebook group and promoting your services on it.

Facebook Marketplace

Facebook Marketplace is a virtual yard sale of new and used items ranging from electronics, autos, real estate, and every item in between. Facebook Marketplace offers you a virtual storefront for your practice. Facebook Marketplace generally reaches around 100 miles of your location. Your Marketplace visitors can view your inventory, ask questions, buy products, read, and leave reviews, and contact you.

Facebook Marketplace is located on your Facebook home screen. You can find it to the left side of your newsfeed. Once there, click on category or *subcategory* to find others in your field.

Facebook Marketplace is an excellent location to show off your crystals, products, and services, including tarot or oracle readings and information on herbal teas. Facebook Marketplace is available on mobile phones, computer desktops, and tablets.

Facebook Marketplace gets your name out to your local community. It will breed familiarity. People will buy from people they like and they will buy from people they trust. If you are interested in creating your own Marketplace, you can find tutelages on YouTube and Facebook on how to take advantage of this opportunity.

The Facebook Marketplace provides you with clear guidelines to promote your business, as well as how to link your products and services on your Facebook page.

Facebook Watch Party and Facebook Live

Facebook Live is a feature that allows you to create live streaming videos for viewers to watch and enjoy, and your watch party can be viewed later by those who were not able to attend.

You can live stream a card reading, a yoga workout, conduct a meditation, or showcase any aspect of your spiritual practice via your live stream.

If you decide to take advantage of Facebook Live, invest in a camera and tripod, as you want a stable view. If you are walking and talking, use a selfie stick and practice your presentation ahead of time.

During your Facebook Live event, ask questions to engage viewers to introduce themselves as you share information about your practice.

If you are presenting a Facebook Live event, I recommend having an assistant to be a second pair of eyes, so that you don't miss an important comments or questions.

Make your events smart, friendly, and relevant to your practice.

Always feature your website and conclude with a call to action such as "the next ten people to schedule an appointment will receive a 10 percent discount" or other incentive.

Promote your Facebook Live Event on all your social media accounts, your newsletter, and with signage in your store or on a banner ad on your business page. Post links to your event in all platforms.

While you are at it, upload your video on YouTube, your website and include a link in your newsletters and in other marketing initiatives. Promote your event, before, during, and after the event.

Don't be offended if people leave before you officially conclude. As with any live events, their departure has nothing to do with you but may have everything to do with picking up the kids from soccer or a scheduled appointment.

Live video streaming is a fun, engaging way to connect with your followers and grow your audience.

Be relevant, pay attention to your viewers' comments and questions, and promote and cross promote on Facebook and all your social media platforms.

Have fun. After all, it's Facebook!

CHAPTER 36

ONLINE GROUPS AND BULLETIN BOARDS

In the previous chapter, we looked at Facebook groups. There are hundreds of other internet groups for you to enjoy and promote your services. An online group is a collection of people who share a common interest and communicate with one another via the internet.

In addition to groups who chat in real time, you can also find groups referred to as forums, where members post messages on threads. A thread allows readers to respond to a subject with their thoughts and comments on the original post.

For example, on Nextdoor.com, if I post a review about a new restaurant in my area, other Nextdoor members have the opportunity to add their comments, questions, and thoughts about my original post. As they respond, my post becomes a thread.

Groups can either be private or public. The owner or group originator is the administrator or group moderator. One of their duties is to ensure all members of the group follow the rules. Rules include maintaining civility, fostering respect among members, and requiring members to follow the group's guidelines.

In some groups, a moderator or administrator will initiate a discussion, and in others, individual members are able to ask questions or launch a new group discussion.

Join and follow groups of interest to you and groups you genuinely enjoy. Groups are a great way to introduce yourself to others.

When joining a group, follow the rules set out by the group administrator. Introduce yourself to the group members. Don't begin with a blatant sales pitch or promotion about your practice. As you post, members who are genuinely interested in you will find their way to you. Let your email's signature line and your comments do the heavy lifting.

Once you are established within a group, you may have the opportunity to post sales, discounts, or special offerings or lead discussions. Make sure you have permission of the group's owner or administrator before doing so.

Even with the sophistication of other web platforms, don't underestimate the power and reach of online groups and bulletin boards.

Yahoo! Groups

Even with the advent of Facebook and other web platforms, Yahoo offers one of the internet's largest online discussion boards.

Yahoo! Groups offer thousands of online discussion groups, and you can find hundreds of groups on every subject under the sun, including sports, child rearing, groups for authors, astrologers, healers, and the paranormal.

For more information on Yahoo! Groups, go to Yahoo and create an email. Look for groups associated with your practice, and join the group.

Once you are established, if allowed by the group's moderator, you may have the opportunity to post sales, discounts, or special offerings. You may be invited to lead a discussion or topic. Make sure you have permission of the group's owner first.

Bulletin Boards

A Bulletin Board is an online forum that allows users to post or read messages and interact with others, sometimes in real-time chats. When I have issues with technology, I turn to a bulletin board.

Bulletin Boards also give you the opportunity to present yourself and promote your spiritual practice to their members.

If you have questions on the practical aspects of running your practice, check out small business forums and bulletin boards to gain knowledge and information on all sorts or business topics, including advice on legal issues, business planning, finance, and accounting.

You can also join and participate or even start your own bulletin board on any aspect of new age spirituality, yoga, crystals, and health and wellness.

Becoming a member of a bulletin board can be a great way to become known in the internet community. As always follow the Board's rules and softly peddle and promote your spiritual practice.

CHAPTER 37

INSTAGRAM

Instagram is social media platform that allows you to share posts, photos, and videos and can be viewed on your desktop or mobile phone.

On Instagram, you can also share your photos, posts, and videos on Facebook, Twitter, and other social media programs. Instagram offers you a number of innovative tools to edit or add to your posts before you share them. However, unlike other media platforms, your stories, photos, and videos will disappear after twenty-four hours, unless you add in a highlight.

Created in 2010, Instagram has been purchased by Facebook and now boasts over 800 million users. I expect that number to rise. Your Instagram viewers can like, comment, mention, tag, and respond to you.

Before you start to use Instagram, I recommend you get comfortable using the platform by setting up a personal account and then follow your favorite celebrities or subjects that interest you. You will find a number of online training and guidance on how to use this great program.

Both Twitter and Instagram use hashtags. A hashtag is a number sign or pound sign followed by a word or short phrase. A hashtag catalogues the subject of your post to Instagram followers and makes you easy to follow.

While you can post up to thirty hashtags on each Instagram post; in my opinion, thirty hashtags distract from your message. I personally recommend using between three and five hashtags that are most relevant to your post. Your hashtag, like all your branding efforts, should be specifically directed to you and developed to attract those to your practice.

As you create your Instagram page, stay true to your brand image by using your colors, font, look, and feel. By using your signature graphics and messages, you will reinforce your brand image.

Promote contests, giveaways, and special promotions on Instagram.

Engage your readers by asking questions revolving around and relative to your practice. Ask open-ended questions that prompt a reply. Open-ended questions allow followers to respond and invest in the topic.

For example, if you sell crystals, provide readers with information on types and uses of crystals, promote classes, events, and how-to videos. Tie in your posts to national holidays and local events, and be sure to tie in your Instagram and all social media to your monthly marketing theme.

You can also post recipes, photos of your psychic teas, tarot or angel card of the day or week, and of course promote any presentation, personal appearance, or event. Offer daily or weekly inspirational quotes and positive thoughts of the day. The goal is to drive viewers to your website and encourage them to set an appointment with you.

As you review Instagram and other social media sites, begin to take notes how others in your industry promote their practices. You do not want to copy others, but you want to be inspired by them to create your own magical promotional opportunities.

Again, organize and plan your marketing initiatives in your promotional calendar, which you will read about later in this book. Keep your focus on the time you invest in each marketing endeavor. Time is money.

Instagram is a great way to promote your business locally and across the World Wide Web.

CHAPTER 38

LINKEDIN

LinkedIn is one of the largest professional networks on the web. LinkedIn is a great place to connect with other professionals in your industry and let them connect with you. You will be able to learn about marketing trends, sales techniques, and how to promote your practice in the real world and online. LinkedIn is not a place to solicit customers. You will be able to contact and connect with others via your LinkedIn messages.

That said, I can assure you new clients may find you as you post positive messages, uplifting thoughts, photos, videos, and articles. You can post notifications on your newsfeed, such as quarterly newsletters or new products. You have ample opportunities to attract customers on other social media platforms.

When registering on LinkedIn, make the most of your profile on your home page. Put your best foot forward on your LinkedIn home page. This includes photos, what your practice is about, as well as posting licenses and certificates you have earned and your skills and endorsements. Include any volunteer experiences as well as your personal and professional interests.

I urge you to join and participate in LinkedIn groups. You will find a wide range of professional organizations in LinkedIn groups as well as groups that will simply inspire and motivate you.

You will discover others in your field and be able to follow others who can help you on your path. You can follow LinkedIn members and acquire colleagues to follow you. When you comment on others' posts, make your responses relevant.

Advertising sponsorships are available on LinkedIn, but remember, you are only reaching other professionals. LinkedIn is a great place to learn new ideas to promote your business and services. If you are not on

LinkedIn, I urge you to participate in this site. If you are on LinkedIn, please feel free to link with me. I'm Linn Random, Author, Certified Angel Practitioner, Archangel Life Coach, Angel Card Reader, Akashic Record and Fairyologist. It would be my privilege to network with you, and I will be in your front row cheering!

CHAPTER 39

LYNDA.COM AND EDUCATIONAL SITES

If you feel you need or want to learn more about the internet, social media platforms, including creating and designing websites or graphics, I recommend Lynda.com.

There are a lot of educational sites on the web to choose from. I like Lynda.com, a wonderful educational site where you can find courses on creative and business marketing skills taught by recognized industry leaders.

Lynda.com has an amazing video library, and you can assess as many online classes each month as you want for a nominal monthly fee. You can pay by the month or take advantage of a discounted annual price. You can opt out at any time, though the end of the subscription will likely take place the month after you advise them you are leaving.

On Lynda.com you can find courses that interest you, and the site is easy to use. You can view your class on your computer or smartphone.

Lynda.com offers tutorials in a variety of languages and will provide you with skills you need and add to your business success. I find Lynda.com a reliable source of information and strongly recommend it.

There are other online learning platforms, including Udemy.com and YouTube videos, as well as classes offered at community colleges and learning centers. If you are unclear on how to do something, learn.

CHAPTER 40

MOBILE WEBSITES AND APPS

More than two-thirds of the world's population uses smartphones to access the internet, and the number is expected to increase over the next few years.

People enjoy smartphones and continue to have access to Wi-Fi through ever-expanding networks. Smartphones are used for calling, texting, reading, research, gaming, music, and shopping. In fact, more than half of shoppers make their purchases on their mobile phones. Our cell phones connect us to friends, family, and the world.

More than half of cell phone users reach for their mobile phones before their first cup of coffee and will check emails before they sleep.

Conventional websites are generally slower to load, navigate, and view on a smartphone or tablet. I have consulted with companies that were proud of their website until they realized how difficult it was to view on a mobile device.

Mobile websites are designed to work on mobile devices. The good news is you don't have to choose. Maximize your market reach by doing a standard and mobile website. Web designers will be able to assist you. Make sure your website or blog is easy to read and navigate from a mobile phone. Give your customers a reason to visit, and give them a reason to return. Make it easy to schedule an appointment or purchase via your mobile site.

Before we leave this subject, I'd like to now cover two additional topics, the Mobile App and QR codes.

Mobile Apps

A mobile app is an abbreviation for mobile application. A mobile app is software platform specifically developed for use on mobile phones or tablets. Initially, apps were created to store emails and contacts, function as calendars and calculators. Today, you can enjoy thousands of games, entertainments, weather, traffic, as well as history and education.

In the New Age universe, you can find numerous apps on astrology, angels, yoga, tarot, and oracle cards. Hay House has a wonderful radio app to keep you inspired.

If you are considering developing your own app, have a clear understanding about how you intend to use it and how you plan to interface it with your customers.

Unless you are knowledgeable about how to create an app for your practice, go to an experienced app developer to create your app. Once your app is available, give users a reason to keep it on their phones and use it daily.

For instance, if you own a yoga studio, consider offering a series of poses or specific routines daily. If you work in Angelic or realms of mediumship, consider an app with information on angels or ghosts.

There are numerous apps on astronomy, card readings, as well as news and information. Find a way to stand out from the crowd and make your app and your services unique. As always, the goal of any online platform is to direct new customers to your website or store.

Marketing Your Mobile Site

The goal of marketing your mobile site or app is to create brand awareness and drive clients to your practice, thereby reaching your financial goals and the satisfaction of knowing your practice is making a difference in the lives of your clients.

Every aspect of your marketing works with every other strategy. Each marketing initiative builds on the one before and when all aspects are complete it, creates perfect picture of success.

Make sure your email campaigns work with mobile devices. Think small for big profits.

CHAPTER 41

NEXTDOOR

Nextdoor is a social network platform for people who live in your immediate area. Think of it as Facebook just for your neighborhood. Nextdoor can be accessed from your phone, home computer, or tablet.

I have found Nextdoor a valuable resource for garage sales, lost pets, notices from law enforcement, as well publicizing local events including area fireworks, concerts, and festivals.

At Halloween, our Nextdoor site shares a Halloween map to guide children to safe homes for trick-or-treaters. During the holiday season, our neighborhood map showcases homes decorated with holiday lights.

In Florida, I have found Nextdoor exceptionally helpful during hurricane season as we come together to help neighbors who have downed fences or those who need hurricane supplies. You are never alone with Nextdoor.

In addition to being a great community forum, Nextdoor is also a great way to connect to with local people who are interested in your services. On Nextdoor you can claim a business page. Business pages are designed for businesses selling goods or offering a service. Business accounts do have certain restrictions; for example, you won't have access to Nextdoor posts from your business page. You can showcase your practice information and receive private messages.

Nextdoor allows you to place your ads in target neighborhoods. For more information on creating your business page, the rules associated with Nextdoor or purchasing advertising, visit your local Nextdoor community.

Nextdoor is a good place to build your reputation and receive local recommendations from those in your community. I would suggest you join Nextdoor for pleasure and to connect with neighbors. Keep in mind, there is a mix of consumers in your neighborhood, and not all will be receptive to your services. That said, every little bit of exposure helps.

CHAPTER 42

ONLINE CLASSES

E-learning and educational platforms have become a $107 billion-dollar industry, and that number is expected to triple by 2025.

Teaching an online class promotes your practice, elevates your professional credibility, and can create an additional revenue stream for you. In fact, it's one of the fastest ways to establish yourself as an expert.

Whether you create a comprehensive class or a series of short how-to videos on your own YouTube channel, an online class will drive will drive traffic to your practice. Plus, it looks good on your résumé or when being introduced at speaking engagements.

Creating an educational program is time intensive, but once it is completed, it will require minimum ongoing effort. You can develop your online course from the comfort of your own home or film from a live event. Students can access your course from their computers, their mobile phones, podcasts, through emails, YouTube, or a Learning Management System known as LMS.

You can offer your course on your website in a downloadable format. You can also post your classes on any number of online schools and e-learning platforms.

Examples of e-learning platforms include but are not limited to Lynda.com, Hay House, and Udemy.com. I have taken numerous classes on all three schools.

Udemy.com is an online learning center. This for-profit education site shares the course profits with teachers. Udemy.com states the average instructor can earn between $1,500 and $3,000 per month per course. This will vary by the number of students who take your course and the promotion you put into course promotion. Be realistic, as even the most popular instructors on Udemy will tell you to expect a modest income initially, but as your reputation and interest in your class grows, combined with a strong publicity and promotion campaign, revenue stream will increase.

I am planning to offer a Udemy course on The Business Side of a Spiritual Practice.

Embed your logo into the video, or prominently place your logo on a backdrop behind you as you teach your class. Create links to your website and post your website on your signage.

If you have a Facebook group, invite Udemy students to join it.

While this chapter is primarily focused on creating an online class, you can most certainly offer your course or courses in the real world at universities, community colleges, in your meet-up group, and at New Age events and festivals.

For tips on a real-world class, review the chapter on Public Speaking and YouTube. There will be more about Meet-Ups in the last section of this book.

Developing an online class is yet another marketing concept that is designed to drive customers to your spiritual practice.

Creating an Online Class

When you plan on developing an online course, first select your topic and create an outline on how you intend to present your information. If you have never taken an online course, I recommend you take several. The courses you take will not only be educational but provide you with an understanding on how to structure your own classes.

Create a topic relevant to your practice and plan out how you intend to present it. As you begin to structure your class, I suggest you divide your subject into sections. Typically, online instructors divide their course into three- to twenty-minute segments. For example, if I were teaching a course on Angels, I might begin with an overview of the types of Angels, then move into the next lecture on Angel hierarchy, after which I would share information about each Angel and finish my course in how to work with Angels in your everyday life.

As you plan your material, you may want to plan a competency test at the end of each chapter, to evaluate student progress and understanding of the material. Likewise, decide if you intend to provide your students with handouts and resources to enhance your subject matter.

Don't be discouraged if you find there are already a number of videos on your subject. There is room for everyone, and I can assure you each offering will attract its own audience with its distinctive message.

When your class outline is complete, as you prepare to record, invest in a good-quality microphone and camera and some inexpensive studio lighting. This equipment will give you a polished and professional look and is more affordable than you think. Read reviews and visit your local computer store or music store. Tell the sales representative exactly how you intend to use your equipment. While you are there, be sure to a select tripod for your camera that is both portable with an adjustable camera stand holder.

With your equipment in place, after several practice runs, choose a quiet time to record. Eliminate barking dogs and interruptions from children who can't find a lost toy. Check for background noises your microphone might pick up, like noisy household appliances or outside machinery. Turn your cell phone off during recordings. Be patient and pause your recording if you hear a siren pass by.

Most online presenters choose an upper-body shot, either standing up or behind a desk. Walking is acceptable, but pay attention to your background. You want to be the focal point of any recording, not the neighborhood cat sneaking up on a bird behind you.

Set your production stage; I recommend you keep décor simple and clean. Make your space presentable and aesthetically pleasing for the viewers. A simple floral arrangement or lovely crystals will do. The focus should be on you and your message.

Behind my computer desk, I have books, office supplies, and an odd assortment of office accessories. For video presentations, classes, and readings, I have a lovely angelic tapestry that drops into place; no one is the wiser, except now you.

Once you have decided on your location, pay attention to your lighting. Make sure your lighting stays consistent throughout your presentation, as you don't want morning light the first part of your hour-long presentation and then a dramatic light shift in the afternoon, unless of course you have scheduled a viewer break between the morning and afternoon session. I have taken any number of online courses where a short break is in order for both the presenter and viewer.

If you are filming outdoors, make sure to position the sun at your back. You don't want to be squinting into the camera.

Are you planning on inserting a slide into your presentation or using a flip chart or poster board? Consider a nameplate, signage, or your logo embedded into your video presentation.

Whether in person before a large group or on an online video, be friendly, professional, and animated. Speak as if you are talking to a friend, because you are.

While you don't want to sit like a statue, do be aware of excessive hand movements and gestures that would distract from your lecture.

Have a glass of water handy, and practice, practice, practice. Practice in front of a mirror or your family, friends, or your pet before recording your presentation.

When creating an online presentation, maintain eye contact with your camera, and make sure the camera's centered perfectly on you.

Your actual presentation should be organized, engaging, and if possible, add in personal stories, anecdotes, and examples. Don't mention actual clients' names without their permission. If you use a client's story, change the name to "protect the innocent."

If you make a small error, laugh at yourself and move on. If it's a big one, rerecord that segment.

Pay attention to time. Time yourself and practice your lecture before you start to film.

Your online class or video will create interest in you and attract customers to your practice. Once your course, class, or video is finished, you'll want to promote it.

Marketing Your Online Class

Your marketing strategy should include promotion on all your social media platforms, on your website, and at any speaking engagements or personal appearances. Promote your class on your blog, in newsletters, emails, and press releases.

Create multiple classes and post them on Udemy, YouTube, and your website, as well as other educational sites. Udemy offers its teachers class discounts; don't be afraid to take advantage of them. What you lose in an individual discount will be quickly recovered with a multitude of students who will take advantage of the discount.

While you want to sell and promote your classes, I highly recommend you offer a short version of your class to give potential students an opportunity to view your style and understand your services. Free classes or miniclasses are a great way to capture students and entice them into enrolling into your classes.

Before launching your class, you might consider a teaser campaign for Twitter, Instagram, and Facebook, A teaser campaign is a short advertisement that is created to build excitement and expectations. Movie trailers at the beginning of upcoming movies are examples of a teaser campaign. Using my example of an Angel-themed class, I might promote my teaser campaign with a question such as "Do you believe in Angels?" followed by a second teaser such as, "Learn how to communicate with Angels. Coming June 1."

Offer an early bird discount registration to your course. Setting a time limit for your discount creates urgency and will prompt interested recipients to sign up.

Post class reviews. Positive reviews encourage potential students to take your class. If you are just starting out, positive reviews will also attract new students.

Have a friend or associate interview you about your class for a YouTube video.

Offer added value to your course with incentives. An example of an incentive might be offering bonus videos related to your class as part of your promotional package. State that your bonus courses are worth $250 and are included in this course for the next five days.

Create postcards and flyers, as well as poster boards announcing your class at your store or virtual posters on Pinterest, Facebook, and all your social media platforms. Make sure you send encouraging announcements to past students to inform them of new classes.

Cross-promote with your affiliates, and offer to promote their classes to your followers and students. Tell your affiliates you will give their clients a special discount.

If your course is pricey, consider offering a monthly payment plan.

You may even consider buying a few ads across your social media platforms to promote your course.

Offering an online course will help your brand and establish you as a leader in your profession, helping you reach your financial goals.

CHAPTER 43

PINTEREST

Pinterest is an image-driven social media platform that allows users to share and post images, pictures, and quotes with uplifting messages and thoughts. Pinterest users search for images and photos, which on Pinterest are called pins. Once users find a pin they like, they post their favorites to their own individual boards. A board is a collection of your favorite pins, and you can have as many boards as you like.

As an example, as a Pinterest user searches for angels, in a matter of days, the Pinterest platform will begin recommending additional Angel images to them to select to their angel folder.

On Pinterest you can follow others, and they can follow you. Pinterest has over 100 million users and can provide an excellent platform to support your brand and increase traffic to your website.

Pinterest is image driven, so keep any messages short. Bulleted information is easy to read and is a recommended graphic format for this platform. Save your articles for other media outlets.

In addition to posting images, you can also use this platform to post contests, products, surveys, and events. Link any graphics to your website. The goal of any social media platform is always to direct traffic to your website.

If you are new to Pinterest, it's easy to get started. Create a profile and type in your interests. Create a board to store the images you enjoy. As you build your board, the Pinterest platform will suggest new photos to add to your collection.

If you are a yoga instructor, you can demonstrate yoga poses or create a bulleted message about the benefits of each pose

If you work with Angels, are a Medium, or are a Light worker, consider posting angelic images or beautiful clouds in a blue sky, with a caption, "Heaven is Real," or state "I believe in Angels." Embed a link to your website to direct Pinterest users to you.

Recipes are very popular on Pinterest. If you work with herbs or promote healthy living, post your favorite recipes, as they are a great way to capture attention and bring customers to your spiritual practice. Post a recipe of the month, and share your favorites in your newsletter.

Pinterest is great fun and a good way to connect with others, share your passions, share information about your practice, and use Pinterest to drive traffic to your site.

CHAPTER 44

PODCASTING

Blogs are read. Vlogs are viewed. Podcasts, for the most part, are listened to over the internet on MP3 players or mobile phones. Podcasts can be copied to CDs or DVDs.

The term Podcast was fashioned by combing "iPod" and "broadcast."

For the most part, Podcasts are audio. The length of an average Podcast is between thirty and forty-five minutes. By comparison, YouTube videos are generally three to four minutes.

Podcasts are generally released in installments as part of a series. They are enjoyed as listeners commute to and from work, while at the gym, walking or jogging in the park, or relaxing at the beach or in the comfort of their own homes.

Listeners have a variety of Podcasts available to them, from informative and educational to spiritual and a wide variety of new age topics. While plenty of comedies are available, some of the most popular Podcast topics are true crime.

I grew up in Japan. After school, I used to race home to listen to Armed Forces Radio. My imagination soared as I listened to The Roy Rogers Show, The Lone Ranger, and Let's Pretend. As I listened to those old radio shows my heart soared as my imagination colored images in my mind. Podcasting, to me, is reminiscent of those wonderful old radio shows.

If you are not familiar with Podcasts, listen to several types of Podcasts for pleasure but with a critical ear. How did the podcaster begin? How did each segment end? How did the podcast keep and hold your interest? Like a good book, a clever podcaster will want to keep you turning the page or in this medium, listening.

As you consider a Podcast, understand the cost in time, commitment, and your return on investment. Professional equipment can run anywhere from $200 to $5,000 for your initial equipment purchase. Be sure you are aware of all the financial costs, as well as the hours to create a podcast. For me, time is money.

When undertaking any video presentation, invest in a good microphone. To find the right microphone, read reviews and have a conversation with those helpful techs at your local computer store. Tell them exactly how you plan to use it and your budget. Keep in mind, the most expensive microphone might not be the best one for your podcast.

You will also find a generous selection of podcasting software to make it easy for you to record, convert, and distribute your work through podcast directories.

If you plan to create your own podcast, I would suggest that you plan out a series of podcasts. Do this by breaking down each topic into a series of at least six podcasts. Write your script, beginning with an interesting attention-grabbing hook. At the conclusion of each segment, tease your next topic.

Most podcasts offer show notes, show notes are companion piece for your podcast akin to handouts for a real-world presentation.

There is a wide selection of podcasting software to make it easy for you to record, convert, and distribute your work through Podcast directories.

Practice with your microphone, and critique your practice presentation. Listen to your voice and make sure you are articulating each word. Eliminate any filler words you use, like hum, ah, okay, and like. If you hear yourself overusing them, stop, because to the listener, they are a distraction.

When you complete your podcast, you will want to select a Podcast Directory. Popular directories include Spotify, Stitcher, iTunes, Google Podcasts, and others Podcast platforms. Once you have selected the directory, follow the instructions to upload your Podcast on the site.

At present, I don't have a Podcast, and I am not an expert in this medium. My expertise is in marketing, but I can assure you there are plenty of books, training modules, and online classes on podcasting, so if you decide to pursue this initiative for your spiritual practice, look to the experts and take courses necessary on the how to create your own Podcast series.

Follow all rules and regulations, and don't use copyrighted materials or music unless you have permission to do so.

If you are doing a series of lectures or talks, stay true to your schedule. If you do not and are sporadic with your timing, you will lose any traction you may have created.

As you consider a podcast, present yourself as a professional, an authority on your subject; for that is how your listeners will perceive you.

Marketing your Podcast

Promote your Podcast on all your social media platforms and real-world marketing strategies you currently have in place. Promote your Podcast on your blogs, newsletters, and to everyone on your email list. Promote your Podcast on your website, Facebook, Twitter, and YouTube and other social media platforms. Promote your Podcast in online discussion groups and on your Facebook community, as well as any Yahoo or other communities you are a member of.

Run contests on your social media platforms for your Podcast and solicit reviews. Promote your Podcast at any speaking engagements and through press releases. Mention your Podcast during any online or media events and create postcards, flyers, and other promotional material.

A Podcast will give your practice exposure and establish you as an expert in your field. Consider hard costs, money, and time investments vs. return on investment. If it makes sense to you, do it. If you feel other mediums have a stronger appeal, focus on other marketing initiatives. You can always dive into podcasting later down the road.

My wish, my passion is to make you and your practice successful.

CHAPTER 45

REVIEWS

Word of mouth is the Holy Grail and the most sought-after form of advertising. I would suggest that Reviews comes in a very close second. Studies show consumers trust online reviews as much they trust a personal recommendation by a friend. Online Reviews are a powerful marketing tool.

Today, Reviews are everywhere. From restaurants to home-improvement companies, consumers look for and read reviews and are influenced by them. Positive reviews convert potential clients into confident customers. Positive Reviews increase sales. Reviews strengthen your brand, fortify your reputation, and set you apart from your competition. Reviews create brand loyalty.

Customers who leave a review feel like they are part of your success. Never miss an opportunity to thank a customer for a great review.

Don't be afraid of a negative review. Consumers trust your business when they see both positive and an occasional negative review. If you have had an unflattering review, reach out to the customer and try to make it right. Others will take note how you tried to make an error right and be more confident in your services.

If you feel a review was truly mean-spirited was posted on your website or even made by someone who is not a customer, remove it. If you cannot remove a negative review because it was posted on a commercial site, offer to make things right with an unhappy customer.

Reviews not only educate new clients about you but can provide you with a steady stream of new business. Reviews also serve as a barometer of customer satisfaction.

I print out my reviews and keep them in a photo album. When I attend book signings or events, I invite attendees to read my reviews.

Reviews help me increase my book sales, and they will help you garner appointments.

If you have a store, display your Reviews in a prominent location and on your website.

Encourage customers to leave feedback by offering a monthly drawing for customers who left reviews. You don't have to give away your services; a small token gift, perhaps a crystal or piece of jewelry will do.

You might want to consider hosting an afternoon tea for customers who leave reviews. Reviews convert lookers into buyers and pave your way to financial success.

CHAPTER 46

TWITTER

Twitter is a very popular social media platform that allows users to post and interact with other Twitter users. On Twitter you can follow and engage with friends and celebrities, share thoughts about sports, news and an endless bank of stories and causes.

To post messages on Twitter, you first need to register as a user. As a user, you will be able to communicate with others in the Twitter world. Messages on Twitter care called tweets. The term tweet derives its name from the cute little blue bird, the Twitter logo.

With your Twitter account, you can tweet and respond to those you are following and those following you.

When you first register, you will be prompted to create a profile. On your Twitter profile page, plan on posting a photo, a banner, logo, and your profile. When designing your Twitter page, remember to size them appropriately for Twitter users who primarily view their accounts on their mobile phones.

I recommend you create banner especially for your Twitter page. I use the same banner style on my Facebook page and other platforms, but each is sized appropriately for each platform. My banner ad was created by one of my favorite graphic artists at FiverR.com.

For page ideas, look at how others create their profiles. On your Twitter profile page, plan on posting a photo, a banner, logo, and a few words about your practice. On my Twitter home page, I have a photo and, of course, a link to my website. Keep in mind the goal of this social media platform is to drive and support your spiritual practice.

As you develop your Twitter followers, stay focused on your message and direct it to your target demographics. Your target demographics are those who are interested in your product or service.

I follow James Van Praagh, Raleigh Valentine, Flavia Kate Peters, the Fairy Lady, and Hay House. I enjoy and retweet their uplifting messages. Follow those who are in your industry and those who inspire you.

Keep your branding and your messaging consistent throughout your social media platforms.

Tweet daily. Invite your clients and business associates to follow you, and encourage them to interacting with you by responding to and retweeting your posts.

Set up your Twitter searches for terms relevant to your practice and monitor discussions that are relevant to your business, and look for trending topics.

Twitter users post and respond to tweets via the hashtags. A hashtag is a keyword or phrase that is preceded by the pound or number sign. When you click on a hashtag, you will be able to tweet and post to Twitter users around the world.

Be mindful and pay close attention to trending topics and hashtags that are relevant to your practice.

Twitter is a great platform to offer discounts and contests.

When appropriate, incorporate humor. Ask your followers questions, conduct polls, and solicit opinions. Encourage Twitter users to follow you, visit your site, and register for your newsletters for information and sales.

Everyone appreciates being noticed, so as you post and receive responses, take a moment to respond to followers who comment on your tweets. It's a great way to increase followers. Use photos, videos or graphics to make your tweets stand out.

You may also want to consider a Twitter chat. If you would like to host a Twitter chat, select your topic, a time, and invite Twitter users and others interested in your subject to participate. With your Twitter chat underway, you can provide information and ask questions to garner responses from participants. Most chats on Twitter or other social media platforms will last about an hour.

You can purchase Twitter ads.

As I am writing this book, there are over 975 million users on Twitter. I suspect before this book sees print, there will be well over 200 million users.

Twitter is a wonderful site to market your spiritual practice, whether you are running a promotion or sending out a tweet. Stay consistent to your message, your brand, and your vision. Remember to keep your tweets centered to your practice.

Happy Tweeting!

CHAPTER 47

WEBSITE

If you are in business, you need a website. A website is a twenty-four-hour-a-day, seven-day-a-week online brochure about your spiritual practice.

More than 2.4 billion people use the internet every day, and for many small businesses, a website has replaced the brick-and-mortar store.

Your website allows customers to meet you and have a better appreciation about how they will benefit from you and your services. Customers and potential clients will look for your practice online.

As you contemplate your website, several key elements should already be in place: your name, logo, high concept or tag line, and the brand colors you plan to incorporate into your marketing efforts.

Your website should be easy to read and navigate. Too much information can be overwhelming, and your visitors will get lost in the clutter. Keep it simple. Make your home page inviting, warm, and welcoming.

If you use photos or images, make sure you are not using copyrighted material. It is Illegal to use copyrighted images without the owner's permission. Violation of copyright laws and could result in thousands of dollars in fines as well as a loss of professional reputation and standing.

The look, the feel, and design of your website should resonate with your viewers and make them feel familiar and connected to you.

When considering colors for your website, focus on the colors associated with your industry. For example, if you work Angels or Mediums, consider white clouds, light blues, and golden heavenly colors. For herbalists or Fairyologists, I suggest earth tones of green and brown. Yoga instructors like to create workouts and poses in front of waterfalls, beaches, or picturesque panoramas. Celestial imagery is always a favorite with new age practices, and library or book themes work will with those whose practice revolves around the Akashic Records.

Make your contact information easy to find, as well as your social media platforms.

If you have a brick-and-mortar store, post your hours. If you offer appointments, make your scheduling link easy to find and easy for customers to book an appointment with you. My New Age business friends unanimously recommend Acuity Scheduling to schedule appointments. Acuity Scheduling.com makes it easy to book appointments, send out email or text reminders, and accept payments via Stripe, Square, and PayPal. Acuity offers a variety of packages from free to small monthly payment plans. Their system is compatible with Outlook, Office 365, and Google Calendar, as well as other GoToMeeting type sites.

When you book appointments, you want to also collect payments. If you offer products and items for sale, get a shopping cart for your website. Be sure your shopping cart is encrypted for security, as well as being easy to use and mobile friendly.

Your navigation bars should be easy to use and navigate. Navigation bars are the tabs on your website that allow visitors to move from one page to another. Once upon a time, on my author website, I had clever navigation bars. As a visitor toggled from one page to the next, my navigation bars lit up with little flames. It made my site oh so very dramatic, but they slowed down the average internet user on my site. If your visitors have challenges navigating your site, they will move on to another site that is easier to use. Make sure your navigation tabs are easy to use.

Other navigation bars should highlight your products and services. Separate your products into specific shopping categories, such as oils, crystals, books, jewelry, etc.

Whether you write the content on your website or hire a professional copywriter, keep your messages clean, clear, understandable, and in a simple-to-read font.

Your Bio page or Biography should showcase a bit more information about you. Be friendly and professional, but keep private information private.

If you offer a services or products for sale, acquire a secure shopping cart for your site. Make it easy for a customer to book an appointment and pay you. If your software allows, and with your client's permission, you can store their billing information and credit cards for future use.

Include additional pages and links to your blog, contests, information about any online classes you teach, and reviews. If you offer classes, provide information about your classes and where to sign up. Show an Events tab if you attend New Age Festivals or have speaking engagements. You can have a tab showcasing your online Press Kit.

Include information on any associations, awards, and organizations of which you are a member. Your website can be simple or as extravagant as you like. Your website can be developed by a webmaster or graphic designer, or you can use a template and create your own website.

Many practices use their Facebook page or Blog site as their website. If you opt to use your Facebook or Blog page for your web presence, that's okay. Do what fits your needs and your budget. Look at other websites in your industry for ideas.

Every chapter in this book is designed to drive traffic to your website and your spiritual practice. One of my favorite ways to drive traffic to your site is through a monthly contest or newsletter. As you promote contests, you will drive traffic to your site.

When someone registers for a contest prize on your site, you need to clearly state that by registering for your contest, it gives you permission to contact them about contests and special announcements about your practice.

Give your visitors and customers a reason to return to your website. Keep your content fresh, and promote any new changes on all your social media platforms. Your website showcases your practice like no other and not only gives your practice credibility but helps you garner more customers and achieve your business goals.

Promoting Your Website

As the adage states, all roads lead to Rome; this is also true for website promotion. From your email signature line to your Facebook page, your contests, tweets, and posts, your social media platform, including your business card, flyers, and brochures—direct customers to your website. It's your business location.

Once visitors have found you, give visitors and customers a reason to return by offering newsletters, special offers, contests, and promotions.

Good luck, and write me. I'd love to see your website.

CHAPTER 48

YOUTUBE

YouTube has already been discussed in previous chapters, but I want to recapture the information here. Created in 2005, YouTube is a video-sharing platform where users enjoy full-length movies, television shows, an array of music videos, as well as a host of soaring adventures, educational and instructional videos on any subject a viewer wants to learn, grow, or be entertained.

Millions of videos are uploaded and posted on YouTube every week. And you don't have to have a million-dollar production budget to promote your practice on YouTube. You can begin with your camera phone and a tripod.

Please take a moment to review chapters on Public Speaking and Online Classes, and incorporate those the elements into your YouTube video.

As with any marketing initiative, your videos should be created to draw attention from your specific target market. For instance, if you are a masseuse or yoga instructor, a card reader or psychic, consider demonstrating how you practice your trade. People who watch will become connected to you and will feel comfortable when they schedule an appointment or book a class with you. People will buy from people they trust.

YouTube videos should be around three minutes. If you are doing an education or video tutorial, you can make your video a bit longer, but no more than eight to ten minutes each.

The goal of a YouTube Channel is to gain followers. You can accomplish this by having viewers like and subscribe to your channel. Encourage viewers to visit your website, where they will subsequently book appointments or purchase your products.

I recommend you embed your logo or website into your video. If inserting your logo or website link is cost prohibitive, feature a banner, or desk sign in each video and make sure it's readable from the viewers' perspective. If someone comments, respond back and always thank viewers for watching.

To create your own channel, go to YouTube, then go to Settings. Under Settings, you will find a link to create a channel.

As you have done with your other social media platforms, you will want to put both time and thought into your profile. This is a good place to include your High Concept. As you create your profile, maintain all your brand elements, including the look, feel, colors, and format.

If you are new to YouTube, spend time researching this medium before you launch your own channel. Take time to view popular videos in your industry, not to duplicate them, but to understand why a particular video is effective.

Before you upload onto your channel, create a clever title and description of your video. Your title, the description, and your tags are important elements that will help YouTube viewers find you.

When making a YouTube or educational video, consider lighting, sound, if outdoors, the location of the sun, so you aren't squinting into the camera. Do you plan to create your videos with a camera or on your smartphone?

Give your video a captivating start. Your hook can be as simple as, "Do you believe in Angels?"; "How to use Crystals for Healing"; or "How to find Mr. or Ms. Right."

Keep your message on point. Be personal and friendly, but leave viewers wanting more, and make it easy for your viewers to get in touch with you.

Promote your YouTube videos across all your social media platforms and create a link on each. The goal of the YouTube video is to drive internet traffic to your website and to prompt the viewer to schedule an appointment or buy a product.

Be sure you mention your YouTube videos and your YouTube Channel on your collateral materials, at events, in emails, and in your newsletters. When you have a new video, send out a notice to your customers and ask them to like it.

YouTube is one of the most popular websites on the internet. Create your own YouTube videos to increase traffic to your site.

CHAPTER 49

IN CONCLUSION— ONLINE MARKETING

It is essential to have an online presence and market your services on the World Wide Web. At the bare minimum, have a website or Facebook page, so locals can find out more information about you.

I hope you have been jotting down the thoughts and ideas that resonate with you, because in the next section, you are going to put it all together in a Marketing Plan and Promotional Calendar.

As stated, thought out this book, don't get overwhelmed or feel you must do execute every concept included. Do what fits into your budget. Set aside time to execute your marketing plans. Be mindful, your time as you still have a successful practice to run.

PART IV

THE BUSINESS PLAN AND PROMOTIONAL CALENDAR

CHAPTER 50

THE BUSINESS PLAN

As you begin this chapter, you might be thinking, why should I invest time and energy in writing a Business Plan? You support this question by stating you have no intention of borrowing money from relatives or acquiring a business loan. If you might even argue your operational budget is nonexistent. These are good points—if your intention is to fail.

Even in this booming economy, studies reveal half of new businesses will fail within the first five years. This number is staggering. These businesses failed because they failed to plan.

Your Business Plan does not have to be a laborious task of biblical proportions. Your Business Plan can be as formal or informal as you like. It can be a simple two- to five-page plan, or it can be twenty-plus pages. Whatever the length, it does need to set forth your intentions, analyze your current situation, identify what elements are needed to start your practice, and outline your marketing strategies.

Your Business Plan will help clarify your vision and create a plan of action for your promotional calendar. Your Business Plan will serve as a beacon of light and hope in those dark nights when you become discouraged and your Business Plan will light your way to financial success. The Universe would not give you a desire to start your own spiritual practice without also giving you the fulfillment of your dream.

On the practical side, a Business Plan will help you clearly understand your current situation. Understanding where you are will give you direction and allow you to springboard with confidence into financial success.

Only a foolish Captain would set out across the ocean without a compass. A seasoned Commander would have not only a compass but a nautical chart to show him the most direct route to that distant shore.

This same Captain hopes for fair weather and smooth waters but is prepared for storms along way.

Creating a Business Plan will also give you a platform from which to rise. A Business Plan shared with friends and family will enable them to understand your dreams and to buy into your success.

If you need assistance in writing your Business Plan, free templates are available online, or you can simply craft your own Business Plan from the following. This simple but clear formula has served me well for over thirty years.

Your Business Plan should begin with a vision or mission statement.

The Vision Statement

Your Vision or Mission Statement is the holy ground on which you will build your spiritual practice. It's a commitment to yourself, your customers, and the Universe. Your vision statement serves as a tangible reminder of your mission.

I have visited numerous corporations and industry giants that proudly post their vision statement in the lobby of their businesses. It serves as a reminder to visitors, employees, and all those who enter of the company's mission.

Your Mission Statement will do the same for you. The average length of most vision statements is between ten and fourteen words, so be clear, concise, and let it reflects your truth.

Begin by stating your intention with a clearly written Mission Statement. Your intention, therefore, is a holy pact with the Universe and the Universe will respond. Through your intention, you raise your vibration and draw your dream from mind into the manifest plain.

The following are samples of Mission Statements for a variety of practices.

My mission is to help others find love, health, and prosperity through the healing power of the Universe.

As a spiritual card reader, I dedicate myself to helping others find clarity, direction, and truth.

My mission is to be the channel to connect loved ones with those who have crossed over.

My vision is to bring spiritual attunement of the body, mind, and spirit though yoga.

Your mission statement can be as lofty or as simple as you like. Your mission statement should inspire your professional aspirations and goals.

With your mission statement complete, let's look at your current situation.

Current Situation Analysis

Your situation analysis is an inventory of what you have right now, including a full inventory of items you have and what you need to move forward in your spiritual practice. Begin by assessing your inventory.

Have you selected a name for your practice? Have you checked with Network Solutions or GoDaddy to make sure the name of your spiritual practice is available?

Are you planning to create your own website, or are you planning on using your Facebook or blog site as your practice's business page? If you are planning to use your Facebook page as your business home page, still, be sure to capture your domain name in the event you one day you create your own website.

Before you move to your business launch, also assess your skills, talents, and education. Do you need additional training? If you do, acquire it, so you can begin on solid ground.

Examine what social media platforms you know, are currently on, and what you need to learn before advancing.

Is your business online, is it a brick-and-mortar store, or both?

Many successful businesses began at the kitchen table. Apple, Google, and Amazon all started in a garage. Where ever you start your practice, bless your space, for your practice is now holy ground.

What collateral materials do you have or will need? These items include a logo, business cards, and two monthly calendars, one for appointments and the other to plan out your promotional and marketing initiatives. Remember, there is no shame in getting your initial supplies from the Dollar Store; do what works for you.

If you can, I would strongly urge you to purchase a good customer relations management (CRM) system to keep track of and in touch with your customers. If you cannot afford a CRM system, then create an Excel spread sheet or Word document to log your customers and potential clients. If you cannot afford these, buy a pack of index cards, but do keep track of your clients.

As you move forward, don't be surprised if you meet a mentor at a coffee shop or find that perfect desk available at a yard sale. What you need will appear, as you have activated the Law of Attraction in your life.

As you assess your strengths and weaknesses, develop a support team in the real world, or you can draw on the ever-present wisdom of the Ascended Masters.

Understand this is your current situation analysis, not your endgame; it's the beginning from which you will rise.

Your situation analysis will give you insights on your strengths and areas you need to acquire.

With your vision and or mission statement as well as your current situation analysis complete, it's time to look at demographics.

Demographics

I have covered demographics and the importance of target marketing to your demographic group in previous chapters, but I would like to review this all-important topic once again for inclusion in your Business Plan. It is critical to understand your products or services and those members of the population who are most likely to purchase them.

Do your demographics include women, men, or both? What are the ages? Where do they live? What is their income? What are they interested in, and what would prompt them to schedule an appointment or enter your store to purchase your merchandise?

If you need a bit of help in understanding your customers, have fun in creating an avatar for your practice. To illustrate this exercise, I am creating a female avatar. She is the archetype of your ideal customer. Give her a name and a persona. Let's call her Savannah. Who is she, and what do you know about her? She is, of course, your ideal client, who is very interested in your practice and services. Get to know her. Where does she live? Where does she shop? What type of car does she drive? What does she watch on television, listen to on radio, and what magazines, newspapers, and books does she read? Does she practice yoga? Does she own a pet? Is she a vegetarian or vegan? What are her habits? What are her interests? Is she socially active on the internet? And what marketing initiative would catch her attention and bring her to your practice? Savannah is a fictional character, but as you understand your ideal customer, you will be guided to the right marketing initiatives, campaigns, and promotions that will attract customers to you.

Understanding your demographics and Savannah will help you focus on the marketing strategies right for your practice.

You probably already have a strong insight into the New Age community in your area, so you have an idea as to what newspapers and magazines they are reading.

If you need more insight into your demographics, visit your local health-food store, and enjoy a cup of tea while doing some serious people watching. Notice the ages of the people visiting the store. What are they buying? Pick up any publications you find. You will gain powerful knowledge into your market by this simple activity.

If there are no health-food stores in your area, don't be discouraged. Visit yoga studios, healthy-dining restaurants, and new age bookstores; all will give you an idea of consumers who make up your target market group.

Also, assess the number of yoga classes and studios in your area and other new age practitioners. Look on MeetUp for groups similar to yours.

Your local library and Chamber of Commerce will have statistical information on your area's population. At the library, also check with associations in your area. Reference librarians are an underused resource to help you gain knowledge about your community. Once you have a clear idea of who your target market is, it's now time to look at your competition.

Competition

The truth is, there is no competition. There is a place for everyone, and everyone has a pathway to success. We want everyone to be successful!

However, it may be prudent to identify others in your field and understand what they are doing well and how you can distinguish your practice from theirs. Keep in mind that other practitioners in your profession can turn into your best business allies.

Domino's Pizza isn't discouraged because a Pizza Hut opens next door. Domino's will look for ways to distinguish their take-out business from other pizzerias in the area.

While you will never want to duplicate or copy your competitors' advertising, you do want to note where they place their advertising dollars. If you see their ad in a certain magazine month after month or in a newspaper week after week, it's a telltale sign that publication is working for them. Those publications and periodicals might be worth looking into for your own practice.

If they are participating in events, investigate those events to see if they are a good fit for you.

By understanding your competitors, you can develop a strategy to make your practice stand out.

Business and Marketing Strategy

I recommend breaking down your marketing plans into two sections, the first for real-world strategies and the second for online marketing campaigns.

If you haven't been keeping notes of the marketing strategies you want to implement, refer back to each chapter in this book, as you are now going to incorporate the thoughts and ideas you want to execute. If you have been keeping notes, great; you are going to be incorporating them into your business strategy now.

For this section, I'd like you to create three lists. The first list should consist of essential marketing concepts you plan on implementing in the first ninety days. The second list are marketing ideas you want to execute in the following ninety-day or three-month period. The third list should consist of marketing concepts you like but for a variety of reasons are on indefinite hold. If you want color code these lists, may I suggest red for your super-hot marketing strategies you want to fulfill immediately; blue for those on the back burner, the concepts you plan on executing in your next phase of marketing plans; and yellow for the warm ideas you like, but due to budgetary, timing, scheduling, or readiness are on indefinite hold for a more appropriate time in the future.

As you record your marketing initiatives, have your promotional calendar handy to pencil in your plans on the dates that would be most beneficial to you. I do mean use a pencil, because your strategies may change during your preplanning stage.

You should have an idea of what marketing strategies you want to put into place. We will be doing a deep dive into the implementation of those strategies in the next chapter, which will cover how to develop your promotional calendar.

You don't need a million-dollar marketing budget to begin. Most of the strategies in the book are labor intensive. Time is a valuable commodity, and this is especially true when you are beginning your spiritual practice.

Select the marketing and public relations strategies by getting the right message out at the right time to your target market group. Be flexible as you plan, as life and unexpected opportunities can interfere with the best-laid plans. By planning out your marketing initiatives, you have set the stage for a profitable outcome.

Operating Expenses

If your business is already established, do a quick assessment of what you have and will need moving forward.

This includes any county, state, or business licenses you need and the costs of any organizations and associations you want to join, as well as hard costs for business cards, signage, collateral materials, and any associated costs including website development, a CRM system, and other business tools associated with your practice.

As you create your annual budget for all anticipated costs in your marketing plan and for those unexpected great opportunities that arise, I recommend you set aside a contingency fund. A contingency fund is money you set aside for unplanned marketing opportunities or emergencies. You never know when an unplanned initiative comes along that is just too good to pass up. If you have a contingency fund set aside, you will be able to take advantage of these opportunities.

You are in this to help others as well as provide an income for yourself and your family. As you contemplate your increasing revenue, make a list of how you intend to enjoy your new income. Last but not least, in your operating funds, include business insurance.

Insurance

If you have a brick-and-mortar store and full or part time employees, most states require you to carry business insurance. This insurance includes personal lines that would protect your business should someone have a slip and fall at your location. If you have employees, you should also have a workman's compensation plan including work-related injuries to cover employees' medical bills, and lost wages. You can get this type of insurance through a local property insurance agent.

We have all had unhappy clients who come to us with unrealistic expectations or requests. As part of your business costs, protect yourself from unwarranted legal action. Obtain insurance for your practice. There are a number of insurance companies that specialize in insurance for life coaches, therapists, and alternative and holistic practices. I urge you to sign up for this type of insurance.

The cost of this type of insurance generally runs around $100 to $300 a year. It's a must for anyone who practices Reiki.

Many organizations and associations offer discounted insurance for their members. If they do, take advantage of the insurance.

With the bulk of your Business Plan complete, now is the time to put your stamp on it as your write out your conclusion.

Financial Projections and Forecasting

With your operating costs complete, now is the happy time of financial forecasting. A financial forecast is an estimate of future income. This is not a blue-sky affirmation that you will earn a high-six-figure income your first year of operation. While I can assure you, the Universe will support your dream, but you are going to have to put in the work.

As you execute your marketing initiatives, you should anticipate the financial return for each marketing effort. In simplistic terms, forecasting is, "if I do this, I can expect that." Forecasting is all about ROI, return on investment.

Your income and growth will be based on the marketing plans you have made and the implementation and execution of those plans. Be reasonable and realistic in your financial expectation of each plan.

For instance, if you participate in an event with has over two thousand attendees plan and prepare around the elements recommended in this book, you can estimate a return of twenty to more than forty new clients. That number may be conservative as it depends on your efforts to make it successful.

Your financial return or number of new clients will be low if you simply show up and sit at your event booth. Your return will be much higher if you offer a giveaway, are on the featured program, make yourself available to attendees, demonstrate on how to do a reading, and so on. The following is an example of a romance writers' book signing I attended.

The event was a multiauthor book sale and signing at a regional bookstore. There were seven authors present, and the event lasted four hours.

Most of the authors showed up and sat at the table as shoppers passed by. In my area, I had candy, balloons, a couple of retractable signs as well as postcards and free bookmarks. I displayed my album filled with reader reviews. I offered a nice giveaway to one lucky winner if attendees registered for my prize. I greeted everyone and used a little-known, certainly little-used psychological marketing strategy of simply handing my book to everyone who expressed interest. After a few minutes of conversation, I'd ask, "Would you like me to personally autograph your book?"

I had, in effect, given them possession of the book. People don't like relinquishing possession of something once given to them, and I closed the sale by asking if they wanted me to personally autograph their book. I sold nearly thirty books that day. The rest of the authors combined sold five. I had planned the work and worked the plan. I also collected some fifty-plus emails and sent thank-you notes to everyone who took the time to meet with me and had their permission to send out my contests, newsletters, and notices of my future novels. My forecast for the event was ten books; the outcome exceeded my projection.

So, look at each marketing concepts you intend to execute, and anticipate the ROI for each. Be realistic, be optimistic, and consider factors that may be out of your control. For instance, the day of your event, the weather plays havoc, and people stay home. Consider the cost of each marketing strategy, and predict the number of new customers you expect to gain from each. Don't say a marketing initiative failed if you failed to execute properly it.

If your marketing plans revolve around your social media, do not expect to reap thousands of customers by continuously offering a free reading on your Facebook page. Do post your contests, your discounts, your special offers, as well as encouraging people to sign up for your newsletter and blog. Formulate a plan that actively drives traffic to your website or your Facebook page.

Create projections for every marketing initiative, and know that as you continue to build on each effort, you are creating a sales funnel that will reap rewards.

If you consider placing an ad in your local New Age publication, you will be impressed if the advertising executive shares with you the publication has a readership of 250,000 people. Keep in mind, not all 250,000 readers will contact you. Your job is to calculate the cost of the ad versus how many new clients you can expect to gain in new clients from your advertisement. The goal is to bring in more money than you spend.

There are no guarantees when placing an ad in a publication that your ad will work. Refer to the chapter on advertising and contact current advertisers and ask what kind of return they had before you make your own ad purchase. If that advertiser tells you they have had no return, look at their ad before you make your final decision. The fault may not be the publication's but the message, so ask additional advertisers for testimonials. Make your own calls to current advertisers. Don't rely on printed reviews the advertising executive gives you

While you are projecting future income, be aware not all marketing initiatives may bring in instant rewards. For example, you may or may not directly gain X number of customers from a single press release. However, appearing in your local newspaper, or a New Age Publication, will not only give you exposure but will complement other marketing efforts and build on brand recognition. In this case, you will gain income over the course of a fiscal year with consistent public relations campaign.

There is no magic mathematical formula to guesstimate the return on your public relations efforts. However, the accumulated and combined effort of your press releases, newsletters, and monthly contests will add into your financial forecast.

Interacting with your customers, group members, and those who receive your newsletters will help you retain your customer base and encourage repeat and new business.

Don't be afraid of adding in a financial forecast to your Business Plan. It will help you to anticipate your financial growth and what you need to do to reach your goals.

For your Business Plan, I think a one- to two-year projection will be sufficient.

Claim your business grows at a rate of three new customers a week, every week. When you successfully reach that goal, claim five or ten new customers a month until you have a manageable client list that gives you ample time to serve all your clients as well as create a steady income. Energized your income with visualizations, affirmations, and intention through the Law of Attraction, you will have a constant and steady income stream.

Unlike the average business startup, you know how to access the financial abundance of the Universe.

Think big as you claim and embrace a financially successful spiritual practice.

You are almost done with your Business Plan. Let's put a stamp on it!

In Conclusion

Your Business Plan is now complete, and it's time to write your conclusion with confidence. In your Business Plan, you have laid out your intentions, set budgetary parameters and projections, and provided yourself with an action plan to reach your financial goals.

Your conclusion ties it all together, as you are stating you understand your market, you have laid out the marketing plans you intend to develop and execute. In the simplest of terms, you are stating to the world and yourself, "if I do this, if I am faithful to my marketing plans, I can anticipate success in my practice."

Have faith in yourself, and remember, Heaven will move mountains for you.

The conclusion to your Business Plan is your stamp of your success.

CHAPTER 51

YOUR MARKETING AND PROMOTIONAL CALENDAR

With your Business Plan complete, now you are ready organize your marketing strategies in your Marketing and Promotional Calendar.

.The twin pillars of your marketing initiatives are the planning stage and the implementation of your plans. Your marketing programs should run a full calendar year to eighteen months out. Organization is the key to your financial success, and when executed properly will result in a steady stream of new clients. Plan the work. Work the plan.

Before you put pen to paper, make a list of what marketing initiatives you plan to undertake and when you plan to execute them.

There are no small marketing strategies, as each layer builds on the one before and provides you with a stronger base for the next promotion.

Don't be overly ambitious with your marketing plans, especially if you are your entire marketing staff. For the small practice, I suggest planning one or two marketing objectives a month. One of those scheduled projects may be your newsletter.

Choose your promotional calendar from the many monthly/weekly planners at your local office supply store or nearest Walmart. If you prefer, there are many free templates available, including Outlook or Google Calendars.

I'm a bit old-fashioned and extremely detail-oriented. For the last several years, I have purchased two Tools4Wisdom calendars from Amazon. One of the features of the Tools4Wisdom Calendar is at the beginning of each month, there is a two-page priority list that prompts me to examine my goals each month, identify what is important, why they are important, and it helps me focus and prioritize my objectives each month. For me it's worth the investment and helps me stay on track and motivated, plus I love the covers and beautiful New Age themes. I recommend Tools4Widsom Calendars.

For many years, I purchased monthly calendars from the Dollar Store. They work just as well, and I was always happy to use them. Whatever your choice, I would like to suggest you have two planners. One will be reserved for your appointments and the second for your marketing and promotional calendar. Trying to combine both into a single organizer will get cluttered and be overwhelming, so I suggest two monthly planners.

As you contemplate how to fill your Promotional Calendar, my first suggestion is to populate it with national and regional holidays.

Begin planning sales and promotional activities around the major holidays of New Year's Eve, New Year's Day, Easter, Memorial Day, Labor Day, Fourth of July, Thanksgiving, and special shopping days of Black Friday, Small Business Saturday, Cyber Monday, and of course, the entire Christmas shopping season.

What are your plans for those holidays? Will you be closed or have a special sale? Will you need decorations for your store, or do you want to plan publicity or sales around those dates? Do you plan to offer free holiday e-cards on your website? Also note any personal dates including birthdays, baby showers, and vacations, so as not to conflict with your marketing plans.

After major holidays, add in popular national holidays like Valentine's Day, St. Patrick's Day, Cinco de Mayo, Halloween, Mother's and Father's Day, as well as any days or weekends that are important to your community. Incorporate what marketing and promotional strategies you plan on executing.

Also, for those in the New Age community, research and understand what holidays that are important to you and your customers. Depending on your practice, you might want to note the high holy days of the Gods and Goddesses, days that celebrate Wiccan, Pagan, or Moon festivities. All are wonderful reasons for customer events, sales, and special promotions. Be sure to note any Psychic Fairs you plan on attending.

Check the National Day Calendar for additional marketing opportunities. Those are fun days to celebrate, especially if they tie into your practice. They include June 24, International Fairy Day; February 26, National Tell a Fairy Tale Day; October 10, National Angel Food Cake Day; or August 22, National Be an Angel Day. There are designated days for every day of the year. Find one for fun and profit that complements or ties to your spiritual practice.

You will also find special weeks in the National Day Calendar. Take advantage of hosting a National Girls' Night Out in September, or if you are into herbs, yoga, or healing, celebrate National Public Health Week, which occurs a full week every April. Invite everyone to your store for free packets of jelly beans on National Jelly Bean Day. Prepare postcards with your practice name on them, and invite visitors to your store to send a postcard on Send a Card to a Friend Day.

Take advantage of these charming days, and make them your own. Have fun, and use these dates to draw attention to your practice. Post these days on all your social media platforms.

With the major and perhaps minor holidays logged, look for months in which you can create a specific theme to draw traffic to your store or practice. Review the marketing strategies you plan to undertake and then work backwards in your calendar to prepare for the event.

For instance, you may decide to schedule a public speaking engagement. Schedule the day you will contact the group's coordinator to find out what dates are available to you. With your date secure, write out a detailed list of what you will bring to the event, as well as setting time to write out and practice your presentation.

For example, let's say you decided to speak at your local New Age Book Store. You want to plan this event for February 10, a couple of days before Valentine's Day. Your subject is about love and how to attract a soulmate. Begin this initiative with a reconnaissance trip to the New Age Bookstores in your area. Visit several. During this trip, you are simply a shopper as you take stock of the books the store sells as well as observing other items like crystals, jewelry, music, and meditation CDs, you could easily blend into your presentation. Pay attention to any store that offers meeting space to customers, and it is an added bonus, if they already sell coffee, tea, or light refreshments.

Select one or two stores you feel would be most receptive to your presentation. Contact the store manager, and offer to give a one-hour presentation on how to find love through the Law of Attraction.

Ideally, you should contact the store manager two months ahead of time to see if they would be willing to meet with you to schedule an appearance. When you meet with the store manager, you are prepared with your topic and will mention the books, CDs, tapes, cards, and crystals the store has on hand and how you can easily promote them during your presentation. Advise the manager how you plan to promote the event across all your social media platforms. A properly prepared proposition will not only intrigue the manager but help her understand on how your presentation will prompt store sales.

In addition to your social media platforms, advise the manager your publicity of your event includes flyers, press releases, and mentions in community calendars. The more you promote the event, the larger the crowd you will draw. If this is your first presentation and you prefer a smaller gathering, limit your promotion. If the manager is agreeable, ask what type of promotion you can provide in their store, such as point-of-sale display popups, flyers, or bookmarks they can offer their patrons. Ask their permission to use their logo in all your promotional materials.

The manager will very likely see your vision and be receptive to your presentation. Ask the manager how you can tie into their in-house promotion of your event, including signage in the store or showcasing you in their newsletters or on their website. Schedule a date that works for both of you.

With the date secure, consider the elements you need to make your presentation a success. You are now one to two months out from the event.

Give yourself ample time to prepare, in addition to preparing your presentation, consider what collateral materials you will bring to the event. Keep an eye on your ROI so your costs do not exceed your return on investment. You and planning this event to make money for you!

This event can be as large or small as you wish; it depends on the amount of time you invest into it. If this is your first venture into public speaking, I recommend you start small. As you gain experience, you can aim for larger events and venues. Keep in mind if you do very little promotion, you are likely going to have a small turnout; if you do a lot of publicity and promotion, you can expect a standing-room-only crowd.

Once, before a book signing, I ordered T-shirts promoting my book and my appearance and gave the T-shirts to store employees a week before the event. We had a huge turnout! I don't recommend this for the small spiritual practice, but if you have the funds in your budget, consider it.

One week before the event, create a checklist of all the items you will be taking with you to your presentation. Gather them and have them packed in your vehicle the day before. I can speak from experience—there is nothing like having your collateral materials packed and ready the night before an event. Not only will you have all your planned materials with you, but it reduces the stress level the day of the event.

The day of the event, arrive early, and make sure the room and sound equipment and aids are ready for your presentation.

Bring a friend to take photos of your presentation. You will want to collect these photos for future promotions and your social media platforms. If you happen to take anyone's photo, have a model release handy to get their permission to photograph them.

Plan a way to collect the names and emails of attendees so they can sign up for your newsletter or a drawing for your door prize. The store manager may offer to assist you with a giveaway.

If you plan on videotaping your presentation, notify the store manager in advance on where you plan on posting your video, such as YouTube, Udemy, and your website.

At the end of the presentation, have a thank-you note ready for the store manager and each of the store employees.

Upon reaching home, record the names and emails into your CRM and send out thank-you notes to everyone present. Include a one-time special discount with an ending date of seven days after your presentation.

As another example of planning and execution, I am suggesting you plan on attending a New Age Festival in December. To obtain a prime location, contact the event's coordinator as early as possible at the festival. In this scenario, reach out to the coordinator in July or August. Remember, your goal is to secure a location on the main thoroughfare to be available to optimum visitors to the event.

As you consider what elements you want to bring, start planning immediately or schedule early September. Your collateral materials can include handouts, business cards, flyers, ordering any signage, and a giveaway item. You will also need a fishbowl for attendees to write down their names and phone numbers for your prize gift, as well as banners, signs and maybe a tablecloth or table runner for the event.

In addition to the previously mentioned materials, also order and send postcards and special notices to your existing customers.

As the date nears, write out and send a press release to the area newspaper, paying attention to the publication's lead-time criteria requirements.

On every collateral piece, on every promotional announcement, include your booth number and location.

What other resources will you need for this event? What signage will you plan to bring? Will you need a tablecloth, runner, or best yet, a tailored, fitted table cover with your logo on it? Do you plan to have a photographer or friend take photos of you at the event? You will want snapshots to share on your social media platforms, your newsletters and use in brochures. Note, if you take photos, have a sign at the booth stating you are taking photos, get model releases, or take pictures where no one's face is shown. Bring a small gift or handwritten thank-you note for the program director.

By systematically breaking down each event into manageable, doable activities, you will be prepared for the success of each marketing activity.

This is important to note: when working with my past clients, I always, always built in extra days, which gave me time for unexpected delays or last-minute changes.

Also, set a time the month before your newsletters due to work on it. Have a busy list so if a client cancels, use that time to work on your newsletter.

Scheduling time for preparation for each marketing effort, not only will you be fully prepared, but it will reduce the stress and anxiety associated with each project.

As your marketing plans come together month after month, the big picture develops, and you will understand how each strategy keeps you in the buzz year-round. Lay the groundwork in a workable plan of action. As I am fond of saying, plan the work and work the plan; organization and planning are the key.

Spend time planning your social media content. This includes the monthly themes you plan to post each month on your blog, your tweets, Facebook posts, and other platforms like Pinterest as well as your e-newsletters.

Once again, I suggest creating a monthly theme and add to that theme each week.

Plan your promotional calendar with a keen eye on personal and professional responsibilities. Take a look at what events you want to schedule, and remember to leave time to recharge and spend time with your family and friends. If you have a full staff or friends to help you, great, but remember not to overextend yourself.

Be flexible in your planning, as life happens to the best-laid plans. Your car gets a flat, your son advises he needs to bring in fifty cupcakes the next day for his class, or your friend has an emergency. Be open to change, be flexible, and know you are always in the right place, at the right time, doing the right thing. That includes an afternoon to recharge your body. If you do miss a scheduled preplanning day, move it to the next day; it's okay, you have built in extra days just for these unscheduled life events.

I'm an advocate of weekly to-do lists with manageable daily goals.

After each strategy has been executed, track your results. Uncover what worked for you, and repeat those successful strategies. If a particular approach did not yield results, don't do it again.

Review your marketing and promotional plan every thirty to ninety days, to make sure you are staying on top of opportunities, trends, and priorities.

By planning out a marketing and promotional calendar, adhering to your schedule, you will keep your appointment book filled with clients and your bank account growing.

Good luck, and remember, I'll be sharing more thoughts and ideas on www.*theBusinessside.blog.*

CHAPTER 52

ASSOCIATIONS, MEETUP AND SUPPORT GROUPS

A long time ago, there were very few national organizations that served the New Age community. Times have changed, and today there are numerous and wonderful professional organizations to join.

When you join a national organization, you enhance your credibility by letting your customers know you abide by the highest standards of integrity and ethics. Consumers will have more trust in you if they know you participate in a professional organization.

As a member of a national association or international organization, your name will appear in the group's directory. You will be able to post your membership for referrals by others in these organizations and be available to acquire new clients who are looking for a member in your area.

Benefits also include receiving information on industry trends, newsletters, e-newsletters, and articles, as well as being able to join in on local or regional groups.

One of the most valuable features is the conferences hosted by these organizations, where you can certainly take advantage of training and development. You cannot put a price on the connections and friendships you will gain through organizational networking.

Many of these organizations offer their members group healthcare and group insurance for the psychic, medium, or holistic practitioner. In fact, many professional organizations require you to have insurance.

There are too many associations to list. through I will from time to time feature various organizations on my blog, *TheBusinessSide.blog*.

In addition to national and international groups, don't overlook local organizations in your own hometown like the Chamber of Commerce and local small business councils.

Meetup and Local Support Groups

Whether you are a startup or well established; one of the greatest gifts you can give yourself is a support team. You may be one of the lucky ones with dear friends who will support your dreams. I hope that is the case for everyone. If you don't have a group to support your dreams, then start one.

Decades ago, if you wanted to create your own support group, you had to hunt and peck your way about your community to build an alliance. Meetup.com has made that process easier.

Meetup.com is a well-established online media platform that allows you to find groups in your area who share your interests. Whether you want to go hiking, find a New Age group, or attend yoga classes, you can find groups on Meetup.com.

If you are new to Meetup.com, visit the Meetup.com website, type in your zip code, and Meetup will show you groups already meeting in your area, including marketing support teams.

I live close to a very large city, so there are many entrepreneurial groups and groups devoted to social media marketing. You may even find a business group that already fits your criteria. If you don't, you are welcome to use the title of this book, *The Business Side of a Spiritual Practice* to start a chapter. If you decide to start a Business Side of a Spiritual Practice, contact me. I'll send you a free startup kit, including suggested topics and agendas.

If you choose to start your own Meetup group, there may be a slight charge. Once you have applied to start a group, the Meetup team will review and must approve your group in order to ensure it falls within Meetup's guidelines. Approval is very quick and usually takes one day. Once you are approved, Meetup will announce your group and invite others in your area to join. They can accomplish this through existing members who have already expressed an interest new age practices or marketing.

As a member of Meetup, I have indicated my preferences and interests on my profile page. I receive notifications of any new groups who start a new Meetup chapter in my area, and I will be sent an invitation to join.

While I am addressing the Business Side of a Spiritual Practice, keep in mind you can initiate your own Meetup group to support your business or new age practice. Now, back to the Business Side of a Spiritual Practice.

You will need to find a location for your Meetup group to gather. You can choose public venues, such as restaurants, the library, or perhaps a New Age Bookstore, if they have the space. An alternative is to host your Meetup group in your home or a member's home. If you use a member's home, show the location to members only.

Meetup.com groups for attendees, for the most part, are free. Some charge a minimum fee to offset the cost of the meeting's location. Many yoga instructors and other New Age practitioners charge a class fee.

A local writers' group I attend meets at a restaurant. The writers' group charges attendees three dollars to offset the cost of the meeting space, and those in attendance are expected to purchase a meal.

If your group meets in your home or someone else's home, I'd like to suggest a tip jar to offset the cost of refreshments, paper plates, coffee, and toiletries.

With the meeting location secured, get a group consensus as to how often your group wants to meet. As group facilitator, the decision falls on you. Some groups gather once a month, every other week, or once a week for coffee.

Next on your group's agenda is to decide how you want the group meetings to be structured. At your initial meeting, I'd recommend getting a consensus of group members and identify what stage they are in their respective practices. Your group will be a likely mix of streetwise established professionals and new members who don't know where to begin.

Start your meetings with introductions, and ask attendees what they hope to garner from the gathering. Design your group to allow members a free-flowing exchange of ideas and goals. Brainstorm ideas to help you formulate and strengthen the group's interests and corroboration.

On occasion, I suggest bringing in a guest speaker. Guest speakers can be print salespeople, web designers, or specialty products sales executives. Also, spotlight with your own members as they do in-depth presentations on their respective practices.

Form an affiliate buying group with your members. Affiliate group members can enjoy discounts when purchasing from a single source. For instance, a local print shop may offer members a 10 to 15 percent discount when making print purchases. All sorts of office supply stores, retail stores, and restaurants offer discounts to organizations and associations.

Allow members who choose to, cross-promote their practices with one another.

Your support group is designed to provide support, share new marketing opportunities, and even organize events or festivals.

Group members will help you get your business off the ground.

The Universe is ready to assist you and will most definitely bring others to you who are headed on their own spiritual paths.

The next section provides you with some general questions to ask or discuss with others. These invite group participation, discovery, and individual prosperity.

Questions to Ask Your Support Group

First Organizational Meeting

As you are scheduling your first group meeting, advise members to bring a notepad and monthly calendar to be used for promotions. Bring a couple of small notebooks or Dollar Store monthly calendars for anyone who missed your notice.

At the initial meeting, introduce yourself as the group facilitator, and begin with an invocation or meditation. Invite all attendees to share their names, the names of their practices, and what they hope to achieve from their membership, as well as two fun facts, including hobbies and special interests.

Either before or during the initial meeting, have each member share their contact information, and have everyone agree to establish a group email list and contact list.

Their contact information should include the following:

Name_____

Business Name_____

Physical Location_____

Phone_____

Website_____

LinkedIn_____

Facebook_____

Instagram_____

Pinterest_____

Twitter_____

Marketing Level (check one)

Beginner_____Intermediate_____Advanced_____

With introductions complete, set the ground rules.

Ground rules should include that members will respect one another, that there are no stupid questions, and that each member of the group is expected to encourage all members' business goals. Group rules should be faithfully repeated at all future gatherings.

Next on the agenda, discuss with attendees the most convenient meeting times, location, and how often the group wants to meet.

With the preliminaries complete, go into group goals and gauge the interests shared by the membership. If your group members are all beginners, you will want to focus on basic marketing initiatives. If your group members are established, focus on relevant marketing platforms. The following are questions and directions designed for your initial meeting.

1. Ask members to introduce themselves.
2. Ask each member what he or she hopes to achieve from this group.

3. Find out what members are interested in focusing on?
4. Exchange business cards.
5. Where will the group meet?
6. How often can the group meet? Once a week, twice a month, or once a month?
7. What time is good for the group to meet?
8. Will there be any costs or reasons to collect dues (e.g., for instance to offset the costs of the meeting location, assist the host or hostess with coffee or snacks)?
9. Set group ground rules to include there are no dumb questions, everyone is to respect one while mutually supporting each member's growth and development.
10. What experience, knowledge, or support can each member bring to the group.
11. What was the spark that led each member to start his or her practice?
12. What marketing initiatives have worked for their practice?
13. Do members consider themselves, beginners, established, or somewhere in-between?
14. What are members' short-term and long-term goals?
15. What does success look like to each member?
16. Ask members to think about the future of their practices?
17. Ask what marketing concepts he or she would like to learn more about?
18. If members would like to have the team's support, and physical attendance during an open house or sale?
19. What is on everyone's promotional calendar for the next month?

Ongoing Meetings

Ongoing meetings should begin with an invocation or meditation, introduction of any new members, followed by restating group rules. Invite members to share a marketing tip and an update or results of any marketing or promotion they undertook since the last meeting.

Members should also share special events they are hosting, speaking engagements they are participating in, and any New Age conferences or events they have learned of to share with the group.

Remind everyone that the goal of this group is to advance and promote each individual member's business. Teamwork makes the dream work.

Based on the members' interest, I recommend a monthly marketing or public relations topics to be discussed at each meeting. I have pulled questions from each chapter of this book. Pick and choose the ones you like and the questions the group is interested in. I am omitting questions from Part 1 of this book, as they might be deeply personal for members to share in an open forum. However, if everyone is willing to discuss the topics, it might be worth a discussion.

Keep in mind that the focus of the group is to explain how to market, promote, and grow members' businesses through advertising, marketing, and public relations and to support one another on this journey. The following are suggested topics, and of course, add in your own topics for general discussion.

Ongoing Group Marketing and Public Relations

1. Engage in general discussion and introduction to Advertising, Marketing, and Public Relations.
2. Ask members about their branding efforts, including their high concepts.
3. If they don't have one, as the leader of the group, you can explain the importance of branding.
4. Ask members to share their elevator speeches.
5. Ask each member about his or her target market group, demographics, and how he or she reaches the market.
6. Share marketing opportunities that are available in your area.
7. Find out what has worked successfully for members and what has not worked.
8. Share media contacts with the group.

9. Are there reporters or publications that best serve your New Age Practice?
10. What types of collateral materials do members use, including brochures, business cards, flyers, and print materials?
11. What promotional products are they using?
12. Do members have recommendations for printing and marketing materials? Can your group form a buying group with these sources for group discounted prices?
13. Do members offer real-world or online classes? How do they promote them?
14. Do members offer contests or prizes? Where do they successfully promote them?
15. Are there opportunities to cross-promote businesses on each other's emails, Facebook, Twitter, or other social media? Can you exchange articles on one another's newsletters? (Remember this must be an equitable arrangement between members participating in a cross promotion.)
16. Are there any marketing events where members can share a booth or simply show up to support one another during the event?
17. Are members open to support one another on their blogs or vlogs?
18. Can you invite others to support or participate in chats, on Facebook, Instagram, Twitter, Snapchat, YouTube, blogs, and newsletters?
19. Can members create a buzz about each other's promotion? I had a tight group of author friends, and when their posts appeared on chats, we all would jump in and leave positive comments and support one another's books and chats.
20. Do members have websites or mobile apps? Who would members recommend for building new websites?
21. Have members created their own business plans?
22. Do members have promotional calendars?
23. Do members engage in speaking engagements?

24. What type of signage do members have? Where did they order it, and do they have any recommendations for signage?
25. Can you create an affiliate alliance of recommended business on your website? This should be an agreement between members.
26. Would members be interested in cross-promoting each other through banner ads on each other's website?
27. If you have a store, can other members provide you with material or a small shelf space to promote their businesses?

Focus on group interests, and of course, dear reader, suggest this book to others.

CHAPTER 53

CONCLUSION AND FINAL THOUGHTS

I have presented a lot of marketing ideas for you and hope you have found value in each.

Once, at a writer's conference, I was asked by a new author how to make it to the *New York Times* best seller list. Without being flippant, I answered, "First write a good book." The young writer said, "I wrote a good book." I responded, "Great, now learn how to market your book."

So, it is the same for those of you who are starting your own spiritual practice.

If you want to have a successful spiritual practice, you need to learn how to market and promote your business. I have written this book to help you do just that.

I will continue to stay on top of marketing trends for you on my blog, www.*TheBusinessSide.blog*. It's free to join, my blog.

I am also going to prepare Udemy classes for you. My goal and my passion is to help you become successful.

Your practice will help elevate the world and help hundreds if not thousands of people.

I hope my words and experience offered within these pages will play a part in your success.

Remember always, I believe in you!

Linn Random

ABOUT THE AUTHOR

Marketing and Public Relations

Linn Random is a marketing and communications specialist with a comprehensive background and experience in domestic and international marketing.

With an established track record of innovation concepts and an expertise in marketing, public relations, advertising, and sales experience, Linn Random knows the ins and outs of bridging the Business-to-Consumer gap. She has strategically positioned startups as well as strengthened mature clients and is a specialist in business turnaround.

Her experience includes all aspects of Public Relations campaign and strategy, including Copy Writing, Event Planning, Media Kits and Relations, Rolling Press tours, and numerous Trade Shows. Linn spoke on behalf of the US. Department of Commerce on International Advertising and Marketing for small to midsize businesses. Past clients include major theme parks, international hotels, and resorts, real-estate developments, and financial institutions.

When she retired the first time, she was the National Director of an International Marketing firm, and in the mid-1990s, she was Executive Vice-President of a major Internet Company and became involved in all aspects of marketing and promotion on the World Wide Web.

In addition to her busy writing career, Linn also runs her own spiritual practice, Sacred Angel Therapy. She is a certified Angelic Card Reader, Life Coach, Fairyologist, and works with clients through the Akashic Records.

Linn wrote *The Business Side of a Spiritual Practice* for those in the New Age industry. Her passion is to make you a success.

Romantic Suspense Novels

Linn Random has loved romantic suspense since she watched Snow White run from the woodcutter's ax into the arms of a handsome Prince.

Her Romance Novels offer readers spine-tingling suspense, action-packed excitement, and characters that sparkle with intensity and emotion. Reviews state over and over that her novels are fresh, with multilayered plots.

Linn Random has been a frequent guest speaker at groups such as Sisters in Crime, numerous chapters of the Romance Writers of America, the Florida Writers Association, the Mystery Writers of America's Sleuthfest, and has taught online classes.

Linn lives in Central Florida with her husband and two dogs, Wally, and Bae.

For more information about Linn, visit www.LinnRandom.com.

Printed in the United States
By Bookmasters